# Community Gardening

Ellen Kirby and Elizabeth Peters
Editors

Elizabeth Peters
DIRECTOR OF
PUBLICATIONS

Sigrun Wolff Saphire
SENIOR EDITOR

Gerry Moore
SCIENCE EDITOR

Joni Blackburn
COPY EDITOR

Elizabeth Ennis
ART DIRECTOR

Noreen Bradley
VICE-PRESIDENT
OF MARKETING

Scot Medbury
PRESIDENT

Elizabeth Scholtz
DIRECTOR
EMERITUS

Handbook #190

Copyright © 2008 by Brooklyn Botanic Garden, Inc.

All-Region Guides, formerly 21st-Century Gardening
Series, are published three times a year at
1000 Washington Ave., Brooklyn, NY 11225.

Subscription included in Brooklyn Botanic Garden
subscriber membership dues ($35 per year;
$45 outside the United States).

ISBN 13: 978-1-889538-38-9
ISBN 10: 1-889538-38-8

Printed by OGP in China. Printed on recycled paper.

**Cover: Five kinds of sage grown in the the Parkdale Community Beer Garden in Toronto.**
**Above: A comfy spot from which to enjoy the Soo Line Community Garden in Minneapolis**

# Community Gardening

# About This Book

In cities and towns across North America, community gardening is flourishing. The American Community Gardening Association estimates that in the U.S. alone there are 18,000 to 20,000 active gardens. The gardens are large and small; formal and informal; urban, suburban, and rural. They operate on municipal land, land trusts, and private land; many are official, others are guerrilla acts of cultivation. Some community gardens are organized by hundreds of gardeners, others by just a handful. Some gardens allot plots to individuals; in others, gardeners work collectively. Community gardeners grow food or flowers, or curate art or natural features. The common element is that all of these gardens are created and maintained by members of the community for the benefit of the community.

Helping people improve their daily lives through the cultivation and enjoyment of plants is a core mission of Brooklyn Botanic Garden and its GreenBridge community environmental horticulture program, which since 1993 has provided practical support for community gardeners throughout Brooklyn and beyond. This book is Brooklyn Botanic Garden's effort to recognize the great work of this movement, but, as such, it can only scratch the surface in describing community gardening today. The book opens with a chapter highlighting the myriad benefits of community gardening and closes with a recap of all the ways these gardens can be vital neighborhood resources. In between, the authors examine specific types of garden programs and strategies. This book doesn't cover the nuts and bolts of starting a garden, but refers you to some excellent organizations that do. At the back of the book you can find these and other essential resources; a special companion web page (bbg.org/cg) hosts interactive links to an expanded resource list.

Greening, sustainable living, and learning about food are becoming top priorities in North America, and community gardens directly address these issues and more. If you are curious about community gardening, the programs that are described here may inspire you to get involved. And if you're already an active community gardener, this book may help you tell your own story, and perhaps even help you strengthen or expand your garden's work.

**In the Community Peace Garden, scarlet runner beans frame the skyline of Minneapolis.**

# Seeing Green

**Ellen Kirby**

Community gardening changed my life.

I grew up in a small city in western North Carolina, but except for the occasional mowing of our yard I had minimal contact with plants and pretty much took them for granted. My grandparents had all been farmers, but that way of life had vanished in my family. However, after living for ten years in the center of New York City, I found plants, surprisingly, a central part of my life. I discovered my roots on a windowsill in Brooklyn.

When I began gardening outdoors in 1984, the location was a community space designed by a small group of people who had since left the neighborhood. I volunteered to help and quickly learned that the garden needed many more participants if it was to survive. Horticulture care was crucial, but people care was even more important. As I recruited others, my role moved from chief (and only) gardener to mentor and facilitator. New and deep friendships evolved. A community garden was born.

Digging in the soil gave us joy and relaxation. Stress melted away. Seeing others enjoy the beauty and wonder of plants was overwhelmingly gratifying. We realized the potential of gardening for environmental education, recreation, neighborhood improvement, and enrichment of the soul as well as the soil. Composting, as a means to recycle and a metaphor for regeneration, became an obsession.

As our garden grew on a corner of Brooklyn, we soon learned about the expansive network of community gardens in our city and across North America. Through local organizations such as the New York City Council on the Environment, New York City Parks and Recreation's GreenThumb, and Green Guerillas, and national ones like the American Community Gardening Association we began to learn about the history of community gardens as victory gardens, children's gardens, and places of healing. Yet the contemporary practice of community gardening was also evolving in new and exciting ways.

In the late 1980s, Brooklyn Botanic Garden (BBG) was becoming a critical resource for the burgeoning community gardens in New York City and a national

**The Richard D. Parker Memorial Victory Gardens, comprising seven acres in the Fenway area of Boston, were established in 1942 and remain a vibrant community asset.**

## THE GREENEST BLOCK IN BROOKLYN CONTEST

Brooklyn Botanic Garden's annual Greenest Block in Brooklyn recognizes exemplary horticultural achievements by homeowners, businesses, and neighborhoods with prizes and incentives. The summer contest is preceded by spring window box kit sales and yearlong street clinics for block associations and merchants' organizations. The judging process brings Garden staff, volunteers, and local officials out into the community, providing an opportunity to meet Brooklyn residents while admiring the greening of neighborhood streets. Above, residents of Brooklyn's East 25th Street, which won top honors in the Making Brooklyn Bloom residential category in 2006.

model for botanic garden outreach, along with other pioneers like the New York Botanical Garden, Chicago Botanic Garden, and the Montreal Botanical Garden. Set in the midst of the most densely populated urban center in America, BBG was already engaged in serious community outreach through its renowned children's garden and its school programs. Supporting community gardening was the next logical step in its mission to serve the public and advance gardening. The GreenBridge community environmental horticulture program evolved out of BBG's Urban Composting Program, and in 1993 I became its first director. Within seven years of its beginning, we were serving more than 50,000 people, with almost 45,000 of those beyond the gates of the Garden.

Individual stories of community gardeners were always sources of inspiration. Once a group of us were judging for the Greenest Block in Brooklyn contest, a primary outreach program of BBG to block associations. We met a child and her mother who had coaxed to life their own "community garden" along a broken sidewalk in the Red Hook neighborhood. With pride in her eyes, the eight-year-old told us all the Latin names of familiar plants, such as *Echinacea* and *Rudbeckia* for the native coneflowers and black-eyed Susans. We took note of the design of bright colors and witnessed good horticultural practice. Their garden was a lush oasis amid broken sidewalks and vacant lots.

## TYPES OF COMMUNITY GARDENS

It may come as a surprise that we included this curbside garden as a type of community garden. The best known types of community gardens, perhaps, are the allotment gardens in Europe and North America that were established during World War II to aid the war effort, keep citizens occupied, and provide healthy and nutritious food (particularly important because canning supplies were redirected to munitions). These victory gardens provided the prototype for many gardens today that focus on food production and offer individual plots and common resources.

But a community garden is, in fact, anywhere a "community" of people joins together to garden. It is a shared green space that is planned and maintained by some community members for the use and enjoyment of the entire community. A community garden can be a shared garden beside a group of homes (including apartments and other residences), a linear street-side garden, or a school garden. A block association might form to care for street trees or beautify homes in a group project, or a social service or religious organization might engage members to practice gardening on its site. A community garden can even be on a roof or indoors. A courtyard in an apartment building with a beautiful garden where neighbors work together can be a place to connect with others. Think about all the spots in your neighborhood that are potential community gardens.

# The Benefits of Community Gardening

Community gardening has been a lifesaver for many people. Over half the world's people now live in large cities. Increasing density within these cities leads residents to seek space where they can enjoy the satisfaction of gardening, grow food, and interact with others in a safe environment. Exercise, stress reduction, nutrition education, and recreation all take place in community gardens.

Community gardens can be neighborhood crossroads. Gardens foster bonds of friendship and support among diverse people, shape the life of a neighborhood, and provide needed community services. Residual benefits include safer neighborhoods, leadership development, and economic revitalization. Studies have shown that crime is lower in areas that have community gardens, largely due to the fact that more people are "out on the street" and aware of negative behavior. Good neighborhood communication systems grow out of a garden; likewise gardens provide a chance for plain old friendship and the evolution of neighborhood support groups.

Community gardening also provides vital experience with the natural world and demonstrates the value of plants and people in a harmonious relationship. It brings nature into the neighborhood with the focus equally on building community. Community garden projects provide open space for people to join together in their common desire to grow plants, improve the soil, beautify their surroundings, and feed their families.

In due course, the presence of a community garden often leads to improved community services, like police support or sanitation pickup, or amenities like streetlights. Turning a rubbish-filled vacant lot into an oasis of beauty improves the appearance of a street and strengthens housing values. Likewise, a tree-lined street where the trees are well tended by a community group affords a more attractive appearance and also improves the environment by reducing heat and filtering polluted air. Gardens can also teach about recycling through composting, helping to reduce solid waste and thereby saving taxpayers money. Open space, when cared for, generally increases the value of property, the satisfaction of residents, and the neighborhood's quality of life.

People today often feel rootless. Families are spread across countries; immigrants find themselves in unfamiliar surroundings and among unfamiliar cultures. Even the plants are very different! Yet gardening can be a great connector, enabling people to exchange ideas about diverse horticultural traditions and techniques as well as work cooperatively and make decisions through negotiation. The garden becomes a place to connect with other people and with the earth. It can also help establish a sense of community pride.

## GROWING SAFE AND HEALTHY FOOD

Community gardens also provide an opportunity to grow food and to know the source of one's food. Many have started farmers' markets. Organic gardening

**Youth are involved in growing produce and selling it at the South Bronx Community Market outside El Girasol community garden in New York City.**

# BENEFITS OF COMMUNITY GARDENING

Adapted from a list published by St. Paul Parks and Recreation; see the full list at www.stpaul.gov/depts/parks/environment/gardens.

## Community Gardens Encourage Community Organizing

- Foster community identity and increase a sense of ownership and stewardship.
- Allow people from diverse backgrounds to work side by side on common goals and share information about neighborhood groups and community activities.
- Build community leadership and offer a focal point for community organizing; can lead to community-based efforts to deal with other social concerns.

## Community Gardens Prevent Crime

- Provide opportunities to meet and get to know neighbors.
- Increase "eyes on the street" and are recognized by many police departments as an effective community-based crime-prevention strategy.

## Community Gardens Support Youth Development

- Offer unique opportunities to teach youth about where food comes from, practical math skills, basic business principles, the importance of community building and stewardship, and issues of environmental sustainability, while at the same time developing job and life skills.
- Encompass a healthy, inexpensive activity for youth that can bring them closer to nature and allow them to interact with each other in a socially meaningful and physically productive way.

## Community Gardens Produce Food

- Allow families and individuals without land of their own to produce food. Urban agriculture is three to five times more productive per acre than large-scale farming!
- Provide access to nutritionally rich foods that may otherwise be unavailable.
- Studies have shown that community gardeners and their children eat healthier diets than do nongardening families.

## Community Gardens Improve Health

- Eating locally produced food reduces asthma rates, because children consume manageable amounts of local pollen and develop immunities.
- Exposure to green space increases a sense of wellness and belonging; therapeutic horticulture provides many benefits in community gardens.

## Community Gardens Create Green Space

- Add beauty to the community and heighten people's awareness of and appreciation for living things.
- Filter rainwater, helping to keep lakes, rivers, and groundwater clean.
- Restore oxygen to the air and help to reduce air pollution.
- Provide a place to retreat from the noise and commotion of urban environments.
- Garden space is less expensive to develop and maintain than parkland.
- Gardens have been shown to increase local property values; studies show that crime decreases in neighborhoods as the amount of green space increases.

A gardener harvests zucchinis grown in a raised bed in the Dowling Community Garden in Minneapolis.

practices, composting, and reduced use of pesticides all help to assure a healthier food supply. Certainly only a miniscule amount of food is produced in community gardens, but people become much more aware through these practices and can be inspired to work to gain food security and health on a broader level.

Wasatch Community Gardens in Salt Lake City lists these reasons for the revival of community gardens in recent years:

- The nearly complete absence of locally grown produce on the average dinner table

- Public awareness of the destructiveness of fossil fuel–dependent industrial agriculture that results in
  - the loss of healthy topsoil
  - introduction of toxic chemicals into the environment
  - the loss of habitat and a reduction of biodiversity
  - global warming and the disappearance of forests

- Concerns arising from newspaper reports about harmful strains of *E. coli* bacteria and other health risks in our food supply

- The demise of the family farm

As people become aware of the environmental costs of transporting food around the world, they are motivated to bring food crops closer to home. Many community gardeners link up with nearby farmers to learn growing and husbandry techniques and increase the availability of locally grown food.

Working collectively to grow food and medicinal herbs is an age-old practice. Within this broad perspective, one might inquire how community gardening is different from traditional agriculture. In some ways, it is not. Community gardening might be understood as a type of agriculture where people work together in a shared space rather than on privately owned individual farms.

Cited as the first recorded community garden of European immigrants to America, the garden at Bethabara in Winston-Salem, North Carolina, dates back to 1753 when a group of Protestant Moravian immigrants settled a tract of land in the western part of the state. The pioneer settlement created a cooperative community garden to grow their food and medicinal herbs. In 1986 this tract of land was restored to the same design as 1753. Today, volunteer gardeners cultivate plants commonly used by the historic gardeners in a thriving project that over the years has included participants from Africa, India, Japan, and China, among others. Some of these participants, like the Moravians, have been new immigrants to the area.

Gardens everywhere remain places to welcome new immigrants. The garden offers a setting where they can share knowledge and techniques. For example, vertical gardening to grow food is a practice of many cultures in Asia; such techniques are extremely useful in space-challenged food gardens in North America.

## INSPIRING AND EMPOWERING CHILDREN

More schools have gardens than ever before as garden-based learning increasingly relates to all aspects of the curriculum and is recognized as a positive outdoor activity where recreation and education merge. Parents and teachers have become more aware of the need to get children into nature. Obesity has become a national health crisis, and gardening introduces both nutrition education and exercise into the daily activities of youth.

Once, in the garden at one of Brooklyn's public schools, I asked a student what languages were used by the children in his multiethnic neighborhood. Instead of mentioning the expected ones, he replied that Latin was used in the school's garden. The children were learning scientific (Latin) names of

**Students from Philadelphia's Blaine Elementary School show off the fruits of their labor.**

**New York City's Morris Jumel Community Garden in 1995, left, and in 2007. It takes dedicated care over time for community gardens to thrive and grow but the payoff is immeasurable.**

plants as well as their common names. (I've always thought that one of the best ways to keep one's mind sharp was to memorize plant names.) In a workshop I teach on gardening with children and youth, we discuss all the ways that a school garden can support curricula in math, the arts, science, and environmental studies. Measuring garden beds and charting plant growth and productivity develop math skills. Journal keeping and story writing advance observation and literacy skills. Just being in the garden can offer different methods of learning.

Working with children in Brooklyn Botanic Garden's Children's Garden, we see firsthand the exuberance of children taking care of their first plants. This is particularly meaningful to us when we do projects with children with cerebral palsy. Horticulture is therapeutic and can have a major influence on the health and well-being of the whole population. Through the use of adaptive tools, special curricula, and trained staff, gardening can become more available to people with special needs and interests. Through organizations like the American Horticultural Therapy Association, best practices are promoted and facilitators are educated and supported. (See page 48 for more information.)

## TEACHING SKILLS AND BUILDING LEADERSHIP

Beyond a community garden's capacity for mental stimulation, there are many practical skills to learn, including most essentially how to grow plants. For those who wish to go beyond the horticultural basics, master gardener and master composter programs provide excellent intensive training for adults (see page 110). As part of these programs, participants contribute a significant amount of volunteer service to local gardening and environmental programs.

Organizational activities such as teaching, recruiting, planning, and negotiating are essential to furthering the cause of community gardening; such experiences are naturally transferable to other settings as people see the value of joining together to tackle issues around housing, crime prevention, and city services. I have seen garden leaders become community board members, block organizers, public officials, and advocates for housing and a multitude of other matters. More often than not, their skills emerged in a garden and gave them the credibility, insight, and confidence to take on other efforts.

Networks, coalitions, collaborations, and partnerships have become a necessity for information exchange, advocacy to protect open space, and sharing of resources. Community gardens can be caught in the changing values of land, and a city that provides space can also quickly take it away. Strong community support can make the difference between a garden that lives and one that dies. Likewise, supportive public agencies can be crucial to the advancement of gardening.

## MAKING THE CASE

*Legislation such as this excerpt from a 1992 resolution passed by the City of Seattle can provide a good example of how to make the case in your own community.*

WHEREAS, the P-Patch Community Gardens have a long history in Seattle ... and WHEREAS, P-Patch gardens create alternative food sources and contribute as much as 21,000 pounds of free fresh produce to city food banks; and WHEREAS, P-Patch community gardening contributes to the preservation, access to, and use of open space; and WHEREAS, the Seattle P-Patch Program has been recognized nationally as a model for urban gardening; and WHEREAS, the popularity of the gardens continues to grow, especially with increases in housing density within the city;

NOW, THEREFORE, BE IT RESOLVED BY THE CITY COUNCIL OF THE CITY OF SEATTLE, THE MAYOR CONCURRING, THAT: I. The City of Seattle will promote ... cooperation among agencies such as the Parks Department, the Engineering Department, the Housing Authority, the School District, Metro, the Port Authority, the Water Department, City Light, and the Department of Transportation to expand opportunities for community gardening; II. ... any appropriate ordinances be strengthened to encourage, preserve and protect community gardening particularly in medium- and high-density residential areas; III. The City of Seattle will include the P-Patch Program in the evaluation of priority use of city surplus property; IV. The City of Seattle recognizes the economic, environmental and social value of the gardens and will attempt to provide budgetary support ... ; and V. The City of Seattle encourages that expansion of the P-Patch Program and outreach should give special emphasis to low income families and individuals, youth, the elderly, physically challenged, and other special populations.

ADOPTED by the City Council of the City of Seattle the 14th day of September, 1992.

## ENCOURAGING ENVIRONMENTAL RESPONSIBILITY

Much can be done to improve the ecology of any town or city by preserving and sustaining open space. Community gardens promote techniques to conserve precious soil and water resources. They can grow a diverse palette of plants with an emphasis on native species to create biodiversity and support wildlife. Seeing green relieves the pressure of overcrowded conditions, too much concrete, and many other oppressive aspects of daily urban life. A person who has opportunities to connect with nature becomes better equipped to act and advocate for environmental preservation.

When New York City's Department of Sanitation joined with botanic gardens to establish compost education sites, residents saw the connections between recycling and gardening, many for the first time. Hundreds of people attended workshops and joined master composter programs. Thousands purchased home compost bins and attended compost givebacks. What a sight to see lines of people with containers to load up with rich soil made from municipal waste—good public policy does make a difference! These programs grew out of the state's mandate that New York City recycle 20 percent of its residential waste. Everyone benefited.

## Community Gardening Now and for the Future

Community gardening is not just an urban practice. Programs are thriving in small cities and towns. Whereas just a generation or two ago farming was a key occupation, today many small town and city residents have no experience in horticulture of any kind. Some towns have lost their rural areas as development and sprawl have overtaken the countryside. As residences are built on smaller lots, people whose grandparents had their hands in the soil may now have nowhere to plant a seed. As a result, shared gardens are developing where they never existed before. Tenant gardening programs in subdivisions and low-income housing areas are springing up. Master gardeners are trained to offer public education and develop community demonstration gardens.

The value of a citywide gardening initiative is well illustrated by Burlington, Vermont, a city of 40,000 people where a public, private, and nonprofit partnership supports expansive programs. The first community gardens in Burlington were established in 1972 by Gardens for All, which later became the National Gardening Association, a public education and outreach organization. Burlington Parks and Recreation coordinates eight allotment-style community garden sites scattered around the city that serve more than 300 households of diverse cultural and socio-economic backgrounds. A nonprofit support group, Friends of Burlington Gardens (FBG), provides technical assistance for community, neighborhood, and school gardens in Burlington and across the state of Vermont. Jim Flint, the organization's founder and executive director, said that in 2006–07 FBG supported 88 garden groups by providing mini-grants to secure amenities such as water systems, fences,

**Youngsters explore soil and soil critters with a BBG master composter.**

bulletin boards, and topsoil and timbers to construct raised beds. To link the resources of rural, suburban, and urban garden projects across the state, FBG started the Vermont Community Garden Network (see burlingtongardens.org).

In a study done by upstate New York garden coordinators, the top reasons for participating in community garden programs were access to better-tasting food, to enjoy nature, and for health benefits, including mental health. The coordinator of one garden in a retirement condominium community described the importance of the garden in helping residents to make the transition from a private home to the retirement community. In urban areas, the enjoyment of nature and open spaces, benefits to mental health, and a food source for low-income households were cited more frequently than in rural areas, while the practice of traditional agriculture was more commonly cited in rural areas. A lack of access to land to cultivate was a common concern mentioned by coordinators in both urban and rural areas.

Community gardening is a life-saving practice. We know we need to work as a community if the practice of gardening is to heal the hurts of isolation. In those cities where there are strong networks and coalitions there is a much greater chance that the number of programs, number of plots, and number of gardens will rise. Protecting these gardens from development requires sharply honed skills far beyond those of typical greening activities. It requires making our gardens meaningful to their communities, and learning how to tell the story of their myriad benefits.

As people of the 21st century, we garden because we know it is good for our own lives. And we also know it is essential, for the very survival of the planet, for people to have opportunity to connect to plants and to each other through this vital activity.

# Food Gardens

## Kat Shiffler, Lara Sheets, and Liz Tylander

In the summer of 2007 the three of us, calling ourselves the Garden Cyclers, took a three-month-long bicycle journey to tour and document food-producing garden projects from Washington, D.C., to Montreal. Our goal on this 1,600-mile trip was to use people-powered transport to explore local alternatives to industrial agriculture. On our journey we met dozens of urban gardeners, organic farmers, eco-innovators, and participants in the growing local foods movement. We saw that the cities with flourishing fresh food programs are the ones that have built the strongest networks to support each other. And more and more, these networks are made up of young people (like ourselves) who are inspired to act for change in our communities.

The "hipness" of local food is a trend we seem to be constantly reminded about as farmers' markets sprout up, restaurants promote value-added farm products, and epicurean media culture makes *local* the new *organic*. This return to local is great for some small farmers, who can now make a decent living—and be recognized as the artisans they are—when tapping into these markets. Keeping it local is also good for local economies and sends an important message to big agriculture. And it goes without saying that the locavore movement is good for the consumer's health.

But we Garden Cyclers want to keep in mind that everyone should be able to partake of the benefits of fresh, local food. Programs like the Food Project in Boston and East New York Farms! in Brooklyn are turning the typical diets of urban youth upside down and bringing fresh foods to their neighborhoods. From Denver to Dallas, gardens provide places for recent immigrants to grow familiar foods. What's "hip" about this local foods scene is that it takes place in gardens in abandoned lots, under elevated subway rails, in schoolyards, and in window boxes in apartment buildings everywhere—in short, any time a few people get together to start a garden.

The following pages profile just eight of the hundreds of exciting community food garden programs now thriving in the U.S. and Canada. They offer a peek into the richness and diversity of successful grassroots efforts as well as some of the lessons these programs have learned as they've grown. To find local food programs in your own community, visit www.localharvest.org.

**Growing food is gaining ground in cities throughout North America, like Minneapolis (pictured).**

# CITY SLICKER FARMS

**WEST OAKLAND, CALIFORNIA**
**www.cityslickerfarms.org**

Founded 2001

People Four full-time and two to three part-time staff; hundreds of volunteers

Sites Five urban farms on former vacant lots, Ralph Bunche School Nursery, Mandela Farmers' Market, plus more than 60 backyard food gardens

Mission City Slicker Farms increases food self-sufficiency in West Oakland by creating organic, sustainable, high-yield urban farms and backyard gardens.

Core Activities

• Build and maintain backyard food gardens.

• Set up markets to distribute produce grown in the community.

• Educate youth and adults about organic gardening, food justice, environmental issues, and nutrition.

Description City Slicker Farms (CSF) was founded when West Oakland resident and local farmer Willow Rosenthal began to feel that she was growing food only for those people who could afford it. She formed a nonprofit to grow organic produce for her working-class community. In the beginning, the CSF organizers let their neighbors know what they were going to do and then "just did it," says Rosenthal. Since then, CSF has evolved to be a truly community-based organization. It has operated a farm stand at the Central Street Farm, its main site, every Saturday for the past seven years, building community support and distributing over 50,000 pounds of organic produce in that time. Central Street Farm also serves as a demonstration site where animal-husbandry techniques (for keeping chickens, ducks, and bees) and different growing methods are showcased and seedlings and compost are distributed.

As with most urban agriculture projects, City Slicker Farms bases its work primarily on lands that it does not own. This constraint is what motivated the development of CSF's Back-Yard Garden Building Program, which provides assistance to low-income residents who grow produce at their homes to either feed their families or sell or barter at CSF sites. Staff and volunteers help plan and build the organic backyard gardens and provide ongoing support and materials. City Slicker Farms provides markets for these backyard farmers and works with them to assure quality.

City Slicker Farms also operates a compost program, for which it picks up kitchen scraps from area restaurants via bicycles. For its nursery and seed-saving program, volunteers cultivate medicinal and culinary herbs, vegetables, and fruiting plants, including many culture- or country-specific plant varieties. Workshops and education programs offer residents additional tools for developing self-reliance through gardening.

Outreach Activities Staff and volunteers at City Slicker Farms know their neighbors and promote their programs via face-to-face invitations, as well as through farm stands, workshops, and paid jobs for community members.

Biggest Challenge Even in the midst of the abundant resources for sustainable agriculture in California and a growing local food movement, raising funds to bring healthy food to West Oakland communities of color is still a challenge. It's critical to do "bottom-up work"—building a movement for food self-sufficiency at the community level while also working on the policy level to change the way the food system works.

Successes The City Slicker Farms market has been on the corner every Saturday for the last seven years, providing produce that has been harvested the day before. CSF has installed 60 backyard gardens with local families and continues to provide the materials and support they need.

Favorite Resources The website of the Food and Agriculture Organization of the United Nations (www.fao.org) provides great information about biointensive, organoponic, and vertical growing for urban areas. Another favorite is the book *How to Grow More Vegetables*, by John Jeavons.

Advice Be brave, approach people, and share in differences and commonalities. —*KS*

# COMMUNITY CROPS

**LINCOLN, NEBRASKA**
**www.communitycrops.org**

Founded 2003

People 105 gardening families, 10 farming families, 3 staff members, a paid intern, an AmeriCorps member, and numerous volunteers; gardeners are from the U.S., Cameroon, Sudan, Bosnia, Brazil, Ukraine, Mexico, Iraq, and other countries

Sites 11 community gardens and a 14-acre training farm outside town

Mission Community Combining Resources, Opportunities, and People for Sustainability (Community CROPS) increases food security for refugee, immigrant, and low-income people in Nebraska through asset-based community development that provides resources and technical assistance to grow, market, and add value to locally grown agricultural products.

Core Activities

• Provide community garden space and resources to help families grow food for themselves.

• Work with new farmers to grow and market fresh vegetables.

• Teach youth about growing and cooking garden produce.

• Educate the general public about local food, gardening, and the environment.

Description Community CROPS started out as a single garden in an empty lot near downtown Lincoln, Nebraska. Today, the organization has 11 garden sites, a training farm,

a community-supported agriculture (CSA) program, and a regular stand at a farmers' market. Immigrants and refugees from all over the world are among those who benefit from the gardening and farming opportunities. Community CROPS farmers have introduced specialty crops like Armenian cucumbers and Mexican hot peppers into midwestern cuisine.

In the city, families are able to grow fresh food in neighborhood plots. If you visit the original site at 23rd Street on any given day during the growing season, you might even run into a group of recent immigrants engaged in an English language class amid the tomatoes and compost.

At the 14.4-acre farm outside Lincoln, farmers care for private land and make a living selling crops to restaurants and at the farm stand. These farmers are part of the New Farmer Initiative, an incubator project of the National Immigrant Farming Initiative (NIFI) to help bring new farmers into Nebraska's agricultural tradition. In a state where industrial agriculture of corn and soy has endangered the family farm, new farmers from around the world are able to make a living selling local foods in urban areas.

A relationship with the Nebraska Food Cooperative uses the internet to link the small farmers with consumers. Individuals and restaurants can log on to see posts from Community CROPS about excess brussels sprouts or sweet potatoes, which are then sold at a central distribution point.

Community CROPS also runs the Youth Agricultural Initiative, a project that connects Lincoln youth with gardening. The initiative relies on an annual grant from the Lincoln Community Foundation to reach diverse audiences of young people, ranging from private schools to juvenile detention centers.

Outreach Activities Workshops on gardening-related topics

Biggest Challenge Bringing together all the needed resources to create gardens

High Point In 2007, three farmers together grew and sold over $7,000 worth of produce; staff felt that after a lot of hard work they could really see the farming project being successful.

Favorite Resource American Community Garden Association website: www.communitygarden.org

Advice Form partnerships with other people excited about developing gardens. It spreads out the work, increases the available resources, and makes the project more visible to the public. —KS

# EAST NEW YORK FARMS!

**BROOKLYN, NEW YORK**
**www.eastnewyorkfarms.org**

Founded 1995

People Gardens: 20 teen interns, 3 staff members; market: 23 local gardeners, 3 regional farmers, 11 local vendors

Site One-acre community garden in an urban residential community, half-acre urban farm for a youth program

Mission To organize youth and adult residents to address food issues in their community by promoting urban agriculture and community-based economic development through the East New York (ENY) Farmers' Market

Core Activities

- Grow food for the community.

- Engage youth in hands-on agriculture, leadership learning, and entrepreneurial training.

- Support backyard gardens and offer training in methods of environmentally sustainable gardening like composting, water conservation, and organic pest control.

- Support local growers by operating a neighborhood farmers' market.

- Coordinate a community-supported vegetable share program.

- Preserve community gardens as open space.

- Educate residents about healthy food and food access.

**Description** East New York Farms! began in 1995, as a vision for a community-based food production program that would encompass economic development as well as a greening effort. The Housing Authority of New York City contracted management of the sites to ENY Farms! Today, the core program is an internship through which each year ENY Farms! employs 20 teens from the surrounding neighborhood to learn how to grow food on a half-acre urban farm. Through a leadership program, the youth also sell their produce at the ENY farmers' market. They also help local community gardeners grow food that also sells at the market, support 35 backyard gardens, and also grow 4,000 pounds of produce for donation.

Many ENY Farms! teens come from neighborhoods that lack grocery stores and yet are ringed with fast-food outlets and liquor stores. An education component equips ENY Farms! youth to understand how food access plays out in poorer, underserved communities, and at the market the teens share information about the food security issues that most East New Yorkers face.

From June to November, the ENY Farms! community supported agriculture (CSA) program offers members weekly vegetable shares at a discount. CSA members purchase farm shares and contribute volunteer hours to run the program.

The vibrant farmers' market draws a diverse crowd of folks and food from the neighborhood, with vendors including small-scale local fishermen offering an assortment of fish and crabs and Jamaican women selling not only heirloom vegetables but also spices and ethnic packaged goods. In 2007, the market drew 14,000 people and had over $6,000 in sales. The market effort developed from the community itself, and vendors accept WIC coupons and other food stamp support.

**Outreach Activities** The market is promoted by flyers. The youth program is promoted both by word of mouth and through presentations at public high schools. Workshops and demonstrations draw prospective gardeners and educate people about food.

**Biggest Challenge** Finding funding for programs year after year

**Achievements** Working from the ground up to develop a growing, successful farmers' market and a strong youth program

**Favorite Resource** Community members provide knowledge, experience, and help.

**Advice** Work with the community itself to develop true community projects. —*LS*

# EDIBLE SCHOOLYARD

**BERKELEY, CALIFORNIA**
**www.edibleschoolyard.org**

Founded 1995

People Six staff and two AmeriCorps volunteers who work with teachers, students, chefs, gardeners, farmers, donors, volunteers, neighbors, and parents

Site One acre of raised beds sited at the Martin Luther King Jr. Middle School, with a kitchen in an older building adjacent to the garden

Mission To create and sustain an organic garden and landscape that is wholly integrated into the school's curriculum and lunch program. It involves students in all aspects of farming the garden—as well as in preparing, serving, and eating the food—so as to stimulate their senses and demonstrate the transformative values of community responsibility, good nourishment, and good stewardship of the land.

Core Activities

- Grow herbs, vegetables, flowers, and fruit trees; propagate seeds; tend chickens; and bake pizza with garden-grown toppings.

- Engage in kitchen-based instruction on the relationship between food and life that combines culture, history, language, ecology, biology, and other school subject areas.

- Engage in classroom-based instruction and discussion, augmented by hands-on activities in both the garden and kitchen.

Description The Edible Schoolyard was started by the influential chef Alice Waters, who worked with the MLK principal and community members, chefs, landscape architects, and teachers to transform an abandoned lot into a place for ecological education and kitchen classes. As part of their curriculum, sixth, seventh, and eighth graders all have an opportunity to explore both garden and kitchen. The garden and kitchen serve as an extension of the classroom rather than places of separate experience, using ecological principles to foster cross-connections in the learning

process. Outside the setting of a formal classroom, students and teachers are able to develop relationships that support varied learning modalities.

This experimental haven abounds with many enticing smells, tastes, and objects. Chickens roam the garden and provide eggs for kitchen use. Fruits like strawberries and figs encourage students to smell, pick, and taste. There's a worm bin, compost for the students to turn, a table where they learn how to start seeds, a wood-fired

oven that they use to bake pizzas made from fresh vegetables in the garden, and an arbor built by teachers and students that supports vines and climbing annuals and shelters meetings and celebrations.

Students use seasonal fruits and vegetables to make dishes that might pertain to a certain country or cultural celebration. For example, in the fall students use amaranth to make a Mexican candy called *alegria*. Children also make dressings from herbs in the garden or use lemon or mint in their morning tea. Students practice reflection under the arbor at the open and close of the school day. They are further encouraged to reflect through journal entries that they write in the classroom.

Recognizing their many benefits to children's education and health, the California Department of Education and state legislature have been exemplary in promoting and supporting school gardens, most notably through the 1995 Garden in Every School initiative. The Edible Schoolyard serves as an inspiration to and model for school gardens and kitchen projects across the country. It offers monthly guided tours of the gardens and kitchen classrooms and hosts school groups from the Berkeley Unified School district. Practical resources such as lesson plans and how-to tips are available on its website.

Biggest Challenges Linking what students are learning in the garden to what they're experiencing in the classroom and finding the time to work with teachers to develop lessons that are enticing as well as applicable to the classroom curriculum

Biggest Success The interest and enthusiasm of the students and the time that the classroom teachers have taken to incorporate the garden and kitchen component into the school

Favorite Resource Partnership with teachers and students, which provides invaluable input on what works and what doesn't —*LS*

# GARDENERS IN COMMUNITY DEVELOPMENT

**DALLAS, TEXAS**
**www.gardendallas.org**

Founded 1994

People Staff: 1 full-time and 1 part-time; volunteers: 150 to 200 per season

Sites Seven area gardens: One is based at an elementary school and two others are located on church property where volunteers grow food for area pantries as part of the Plot Against Hunger project. Three neighborhood gardens serve primarily Cambodian and Lao families. Staff members of Gardeners in Community Development (GICD) conduct their business in the gardens, without office space.

Mission "Growing people." Each year GICD makes it possible for hundreds of Dallas-area families, mostly low-income, to enjoy fresh vegetables, herbs, fruits, and flowers grown in area community gardens. These gardens enhance the quality of life for residents in many ways and provide a place to learn and share a joy of gardening with others.

Core Activities

• Grow food with community gardeners.

• Help families sell produce in a market garden.

• Provide training sessions.

• Distribute produce to food pantries.

**Description** The gardens that GICD supports impart gardening know-how to a community and by doing so improve the quality of life in Dallas neighborhoods. With support from Heifer International, GICD conducted 33 training sessions in 2006 on everything from canning to composting to seed saving.

Produce is sold at the East Dallas Community and Market Garden each weekend and early mornings on weekdays. Proceeds from the market benefit refugee gardeners. Many families receive fresh produce from the Plot Against Hunger program. Each year GICD gardeners work with other Dallas programs to deliver more than 7,000 pounds of produce to emergency food providers.

In July 2007, Our Saviour, a four-acre church-based GICD garden in southwest Dallas, was selected to receive a 2,000-gallon water-catchment system and pavilion through the Organic Gardening Magazine Waterworks program (the only garden so recognized in Texas). The tin roof of the outdoor pavilion channels rainwater to the system, while the pavilion itself offers an outdoor learning and social gathering place.

GICD's Hope Garden is certified as a Texas Discovery Gardens Butterfly Habitat, providing the proper host plants, nectar sources, and environmental conditions for all stages of a butterfly's lifecycle. Hope Garden is also certified as Wildlife Habitat by the National Wildlife Federation.

Gardeners in Community Development continues to harvest fresh, healthy produce and provides the spaces to learn and grow to be better gardeners—and better people. As with many community garden projects, the challenge is finding funding, but GICD has survived and grown over 13 years of supporting community development through gardens.

**Outreach Activities** Among GICD's outreach efforts are an annual newsletter, frequent e-newsletters, one-on-one consulting for beginning gardens, and workshops and training sessions.

**Biggest Challenges** Finding official support and recognition for projects from cities, counties, and other infrastructures. It is also a challenge to raise money, and as a result the garden has worked with unpaid or partially paid staff.

**Proudest Moments** For two years in a row, GICD won Heifer International's Passing on the Gift award for the number of pounds donated to food pantries from its gardens and the amount of training offered to the public.

**Advice** Always make sure that what you're doing is something that benefits somebody else. Do the best you can with what you've got. Never give up. —*LT*

# GROWING POWER

**CHICAGO, ILLINOIS; MILWAUKEE, WISCONSIN**
**www.growingpower.org**

Founded 1982

People Staff: 15 each in Chicago and Milwaukee; paid interns

Sites Six farms and many related sites in Chicago and Milwaukee

Mission Growing Power inspires communities to build sustainable food systems that are equitable and ecologically sound, creating a just world, one food-secure community at a time.

Core Activities

• Train people through on-site workshops and hands-on tutorials.

• Network, which involves everything from assisting farmers to helping communities that want to transform city lots into gardens and urban farms.

• Assist individuals in growing commercially in urban areas.

• Produce food.

Description In 1982, Will Allen, Growing Power's founder and executive director, used money earned from his professional basketball career to buy Milwaukee's last working

farm. On that original two acres northeast of Milwaukee, Allen and staff now operate a community food center—the first of its kind in the nation—where seven greenhouses, training gardens, a kitchen, farm animals, aquaculture facilities, and a food distribution center all contribute to a healthy local food system.

Their work is successful thanks to many local partnerships in both Milwaukee and Chicago. Much of what they do involves low-income youth. Through a partnership with the Boys and Girls Club of Greater Milwaukee, 25 students are enrolled in a nutrition and gardening program for two hours a week over four months. In Chicago there is a parallel youth program in which gardening is used as a hands-on teaching tool and job-training opportunity. Growing

Power also participates in local food policy councils and operates a CSA-style food distribution program for low-income residents.

The organization serves as a clearinghouse for urban agriculture training in the Midwest; in 2007 it trained nine people from various parts of the country through its intensive Commercial Sustainable Urban Agriculture program. Workshops range from brief introductions to multiday hands-on lessons in aquaculture, vermiculture, and food processing. After participating in a Growing Power training, individuals draw on acquired skills to start community-based collaborative entrepreneurial projects. Growing Power currently supports ten such projects, including the Market Basket food distribution networks in Chicago and Milwaukee; a cut-flower operation in the low-income neighborhood of Walnut Way, in Milwaukee; and the Rainbow Farmer's Cooperative, which connects producers of farm products to restaurants and markets.

Growing Power wants to see everyone on earth have access to safe, healthy, and affordable food. Says Will Allen, "There's really no success until we're able to put ourselves out of business."

**Outreach Activities** Word of mouth from the 5,000 people a year from all over the world who visit the Milwaukee site and tour the facilities

**Biggest Challenges** Engaging with and working within diverse communities; finding the funds to pay staff enough to sustain them; team building with 30 people in different places; and developing relationships with other organizations

**Favorite Resource** Individual relationships

**Advice** Remember the Ps: Pride, Patience, Passion, Performance, Perseverance, Partners, and Play. Celebrate your victories. To be successful, you have to be in it for the long term. —*KS*

# INTERVALE CENTER

**BURLINGTON, VERMONT**
**www.intervale.org**

Founded 1986

People Staff: 20 (not including farmers, youth interns, and volunteers)

Site 350 acres of farm and conservation land hosting 12 farms

Mission To develop farm- and land-based enterprises that generate economic and social opportunity while protecting natural resources

Core Activities

- Compost Burlington's commercial and residential organic waste.
- Administer Healthy City, a youth program providing training in food production and entrepreneurial skills.
- Provide agriculture-development services and incubator system for beginning farmers.
- Grow trees and shrubs in the conservation nursery for restoration projects.
- Develop a food enterprise center (with the City of Burlington) using sustainable practice for local added-value food processing and distribution.

Description Begun in 1990, the Intervale Farms program supports small-scale beginner farmers through an incubator system, leasing land and necessary agricultural equipment. It also assists with business planning and market access to help independent farms establish the financial foundation for a viable agricultural business. These small farms operate in the same vicinity, allowing a cooperative, mentoring community to develop. Over the first three years, the farmer receives coaching in setting up a business plan while the Intervale Center subsidizes costs of equipment, land, and facilities. After the three-year mark, the center gradually applies the realistic cost of land and resources while assisting the young farmer either to move out to buy his/her own farm and business or to stay at the center and become a mentor to new farmers. Currently 12 farms cultivate 120 acres of land, growing everything from specialty crops for fine dining to greens sold at the farmers' market and local CSA.

Intervale's compost facilities surpass most urban waste treatment centers. Intervale composts 20,000 tons of waste from Burlington's commercial and residential debris. It collects dairy residuals from large companies like Ben and Jerry's and IBM as well as food waste from schools and restaurants and returns rich humus back to the community, in the form of finished compost products sold at the Intervale Center or delivered in bulk by its purple biodiesel-fueled truck. With a catchy motto like "Don't Treat Your Soil Like Dirt," how could any sustainable agriculture advocate not be smitten?

As part of Intervale's Healthy City youth program, teens from the North End neighborhood of Burlington are paid to work 20 hours a week, during which they develop a business plan, grow produce, and then sell it at the farmers' market. The program is expanding to include a greenhouse so that year-round work is available. Healthy City youth also participate in a gleaning and food-distribution program; each year they collect 30,000 pounds of fresh, organic produce to distribute to approximately 20 social service agencies. The goal of this program is to educate youth while connecting the lower-income neighborhoods of Burlington with fresh produce and Intervale's small-scale farmers.

Intervale also runs a garden supply store and promotes public use of the wildlife corridors along the Winooski River on hike and bike trails. Currently, in partnership with the Burlington municipality, it is planning the Food Enterprise Center, "a combination of fresh food production, value-added food processing, green energy use, and social enterprise."

**Biggest Challenge** Fund-raising; the center generates 20 percent of its funds through farm sales and relies on grants and donations for the remaining 80 percent.

**Biggest Successes** Successful small farmers (and seeing kids eat kale!)

**Favorite Resources** The land—the farmers—the veggies

**Advice** Support your local farm— eat local! —*LS*

# NUESTRAS RAÍCES

**HOLYOKE, MASSACHUSETTS**
www.nuestras-raices.org
www.nuestrasraicesfarm.com

Founded 1992

People 100 families, 7 adult staff, and 9 paid youth staff

Sites Two youth gardens; eight community gardens; a multiuse space including a restaurant, bakery, library, greenhouse, and offices; and a 26-acre farm on the Connecticut River

Mission Nuestras Raíces is a grass-roots organization that promotes economic, human, and community development in Holyoke, Massachusetts, through projects relating to food, agriculture, and the environment.

## Core Activities

- Establish and support community gardens.

- Foster enterprise development; women's and youth leadership training.

- Support environmental justice organizing.

- Operate the Tierra de Oportunidades Project, which incubates businesses and offers farmer training, youth development, and environmental conservation and stewardship programs.

Description Nuestras Raíces started more than 15 years ago in a low-income, primarily Latino neighborhood in Holyoke, Massachusetts. Many of the older gardeners grew up farming in Puerto Rico, and through Nuestras Raíces's intergenerational programs have a space to pass along their knowledge to a generation that is removed from that part of their heritage. Some families sell their produce at local markets, and all benefit from improved nutrition and access to fresh, local, and culturally important foods like pumpkins, cilantro, and Puerto Rican sweet peppers.

Nuestras Raíces comprises ten gardens in the city and the 26-acre Caribbean-themed farm project that is home to nature trails, a petting zoo, horse stable, outdoor stage, and farm stand. It has been able to gain access to these lands through partnerships with the city and nonprofit landowners.

Nuestras Raíces has had a large impact on the physical environment of Holyoke: Sites once covered with garbage, needles, and rubble from abandoned homes now offer healthy places for families to grow food and kids to play.

The Centro Agrícola Project, formerly an abandoned building, is now a multiuse space with a restaurant, outdoor plaza, library, greenhouse, bakery, and the main offices for Nuestras Raíces. Program offerings focus on women's leadership, youth development, and environmental justice for impoverished communities. Nuestras Raíces has been able to do this with funding support from various USDA programs; the EPA; state programs for agriculture, culture, and conservation; and private foundations. There is also earned income from the community enterprises that it supports.

**Outreach Activities** Community festivals such as the Festival de la Cosecha (Harvest Festival), combining agricultural themes and Puerto Rican culture; music and cultural events at the farm, restaurant, and bakery; partnerships with health centers, churches, and local colleges and universities

**Biggest Challenge** Building confidence, unity, and strength in a community that has long felt disenfranchised

**Proudest Moments** There are many: harvest time in the gardens; transforming a vacant building into our Centro Agrícola community agricultural center; opening the 30-acre Nuestras Raíces Farm; when Candido Nieves, who entered the youth program at age 9, became a staff member.

**Favorite Resource** The wisdom of older community gardeners

**Advice** The leadership and decision makers of an organization should be made up of the people most impacted by the efforts of the organization. —*KS*

# Small Is Beautiful: Youth Garden Programs

**Patsy Benveniste, Eliza Fournier, Lynne Haynor, and Angela Mason**

Community gardens occupy hallowed space in the American tradition as symbols of civic engagement and beautification, shared endeavor, and hope for a better tomorrow. From the Food Project in Boston's Roxbury neighborhood to the Red Hook Community Farm in Brooklyn, from the Neighborhood Gardens Association in Philadelphia to the Learning Garden at Venice High School in Los Angeles, and from Austin's Sunshine Community Gardens to Seattle's P-Patches, the country is experiencing a resurgence of community-based gardening efforts, especially programs that target youth.

Much credit for this is due to a mounting national demand for locally and sustainably grown food, fired by a full-fledged recognition—anchored in the popular consciousness by Richard Louv's 2006 book *Last Child in the Woods*—that our nation's young people are separated as never before from nature. Thirty-five years ago, in his collection of essays on the subject of sustainability, *Small Is Beautiful*, economist E.F. Schumacher lamented that education was understood and practiced in our age as the process of creating "know-how." "The task of education," Schumacher countered, "would be, first and foremost, the transmission of ideas of value, of what to do with our lives."

Engaging youth in gardens of all types is a way to explore ideas of value and what to do with life in a small-is-beautiful way. It could be the framework for a whole new approach to educating all children.

## Food Systems

Food is a cornerstone from which communities can take on social, cultural, and environmental challenges. Food systems awareness goes far beyond nutrition and encompasses such issues as food access, culturally important foods, food origins, different growing techniques, and food production and distribution. While many young people are exposed to nutrition education in school, few are aware of food systems and their social and environmental impacts. Nutrition education's often prescriptive approach easily turns youth off to learning more about the foods they eat; nevertheless, they still need to make knowledgeable decisions about their food

**Youth harvesting greens at Red Hook Community Farm, a project of Added Value in Brooklyn.**

consumption. Involving teens in their local food system allows them to learn in a hands-on and exploratory manner about food and all aspects of the system that brings food to their families' tables. Community gardens can play the unique role of giving young people a venue for developing a food system from the ground up by growing, preparing, and distributing food in their community.

## GROWING FOOD WITH YOUTH

When we're hungry, we're naturally more concerned with filling our empty bellies than examining the origins of our food. When we go shopping, it's easy to forget how many people and steps are involved in bringing our food to us—we see food as a packaged product available in a supermarket. Growing food plants with young people allows them to form new associations with familiar products. For kids who haven't grown vegetables, carrots conjure images of bite-sized orange sticks in a plastic bag, but for gardeners, carrots are living plants associated with images of tiny seeds, heirloom varieties, or pulling carrots with a friend. Most gardeners have witnessed the wonder of a seed germinating and experienced pride in tending it from sprout to mature plant. When the plant is grown to feed people, another layer of purpose is added. Participating in an outdoor hands-on learning activity where their success helps others can be a very powerful experience for youth of all ages who may not feel empowered in other areas of their lives.

## LEARNING ACTIVITIES

Many curricula and resource guides provide activities that can enrich and deepen students' experience and their understanding of food and food systems, including conventional, organic, and local models and their overlap. For middle-school-aged youth, the Growing Food section of the Linking Food and the Environment (LiFE) curriculum, developed by the Teachers College at Columbia University, has inquiry-based food system lessons that are very accessible for children and facilitators. Older kids would benefit from workshops in the Food Project publication *French Fries and the Food System: A Year-round Curriculum Connecting Youth with Farming and Food*. This guide has lessons for every season that are useful for connecting youth with food and food systems. (See bbg.org/cg for links to these as well as additional resources.)

While learning about food production is an excellent way of raising kids' consciousness about the food they eat, simply asking students to taste the food they are growing offers learning opportunities. For example, people are often reluctant to try food that hasn't been washed (a good policy). This is a great time to ask a few pointed questions to begin a discussion about pesticides, microbes, and lead contamination: Why do we wash our food? Why is it bad to have dirt on our food? What other things might we not want to eat?

The incorporation of wholesome, nutritious food into everyday garden rituals can be a way to encourage further exploration of the food kids grow in the garden. Sub-

**An intern at FoodShare's Urban Agriculture program harvests the first bunch of carrots at an urban farm in Toronto.**

stituting fresh produce and other healthy snacks for traditional "reward" foods like candy and soda can help to do the following:

- **Encourage youth to try new foods.**
- **Initiate dialogue** about what healthy foods are and where they come from.
- **Enhance workshop lessons with real-life experiences** with locally grown, organic, and other nutritious food.

## GREEN YOUTH FARM: CONNECTING KIDS AND COMMUNITY

Like other endeavors of its kind around the country, Chicago Botanic Garden's Green Youth Farm program promotes the multifaceted appeal of gardening to attract teens and better connect with their varying interests, learning styles, and talents. Participation in the Green Youth Farm means being part of a rich experience of exploring gardening through cooking, art, communications training, team building, leadership development, and entrepreneurship. In all these activities, there is a place where each student can achieve and shine.

The heart of the Green Youth Farm experience, combining hands-on tasks with agriculture workshops, links students to their immediate community and to a broader social agenda that looks critically at health, economics, and social justice questions. Green Youth Farm students develop an appreciation of where food comes from, how it

**Youth participants in the Council on the Environment's Learn It, Grow It, Eat It program in New York City grow vegetables and improve food access in their schools and communities.**

gets to their table, and why it is important to look at food and food systems critically. They quickly come to understand that what they grow and what they know through the Green Youth Farm can improve the lives of people in their community and beyond.

Green Youth Farm encourages students to enjoy the food grown by offering solar oven snacks, community lunches, and celebrations. Snacks prepared in homemade solar ovens are a way to incorporate healthy treats straight from the garden as well as introduce the concept of alternative energy sources. Community lunches prepared by student crews for all staff and student workers have become an essential part of the weekly routine at the Green Youth Farm. These lunches help kids learn new ways to prepare produce; celebrate the week's harvest; and appreciate the creativity, service, and work that their peers put into making the meal. Finally, experiencing food as a central part of farm celebrations can be enlightening for youth and others who appreciate and use the garden. There is almost nothing to compare with the pride resulting from a well-cooked meal using home-grown food and sharing it with people who recognize its value.

## LOCAL FOOD DISTRIBUTION

Recognizing the part that the community garden or urban farm plays in the regional food system can be one of the most challenging concepts for young people to grasp. Participation in many levels of the food delivery system is one way to illustrate the importance of the small-scale food producer. Weekly farm stands, small produce subscription services, or community farmers' markets are all ways that youth can be a part of the regional food system. When youth set goals and record harvests and sales, they will see that they can actually help change food systems.

## Team Building and Leadership Development

Gardening with youth provides an excellent way to explore the social development of young people within their communities. Often the mission of a collaborative garden reaches beyond neighborhood beautification or food production and aims to strengthen and unite a community. The power of gardens to bring together people of diverse ages, backgrounds, and interests make them a natural place to build stronger bonds between participants. Team building can motivate young people in particular and set the stage for constructive collaboration with other youth and adults. While team-building exercises aim to foster a more cohesive and motivated gardening group, long-term garden sustainability depends upon directly involving teens in the stewardship of community gardens. Young people need to be given the responsibility of leadership rather than being enlisted merely as helpers in garden projects. By investing in youth leadership skills, gardens can serve the community and prepare youth for success.

### FOSTERING COOPERATION AND LEADERSHIP IN THE GARDEN

Team-building exercises and leadership development in tandem with garden work are excellent tools for achieving your garden's objectives while involving kids. Building community and fostering leadership successfully demand foresight and patience and depend upon the following:

- **Creating a safe space** where all participants feel at ease. Safety can be physical, mental, or emotional, and maintaining a safe space is a continuous endeavor. Establishing community values as a group can often be a first step toward creating a safe space.

- **Treating youth as full participants** whose feelings, thoughts, insights, strengths, and experiences are valued.

- **Providing appropriate supports and challenges** by allowing youth to take risks

**Baskets of CSA vegetables grown by Green Youth Farm are testaments to teamwork.**

A youth instructor at Nuestras Raíces in Holyoke, Massachusetts. For many young people, being trusted with a leadership role may be a transformative experience.

and make mistakes while recognizing that they may need emotional, physical, intellectual, and logistical support to achieve a successful outcome.

- **Reading your group** and adjusting activities or responsibilities for people of different ages, sizes, interests, and energy levels.

- **Leading with genuine enthusiasm** and inspiring others to participate in earnest.

## TEAM BUILDING

Team building can be practiced in myriad ways. Games and activities for breaking the ice, getting to know others, developing interpersonal skills, exploring serious issues, or just having fun can play a large role in community building. Adapting activities for your garden can serve as an excellent tool for resolving specific issues facing your group. For example, your garden may comprise a volunteer base of older community members and teens who feel they share nothing in common. A team-building activity at each morning meeting could establish a common ground. There are many excellent team-building manuals full of games, exercises, puzzles, and discussion prompters. These fun activities are designed to serve as nonthreatening ways to address serious issues such as appreciating diversity, communicating effectively, building trust, promoting healthy group dynamics, and fostering different leadership styles.

While challenging and engaging youth is one component of team building, clarifying goals and celebrating achievement in your garden are also essential to sustaining kids' involvement and a sense of community. Making gardening fun may initially attract young people, but including them in meaningful work opportunities will more fully cultivate their interest. One way to include youth is to collectively set goals and illustrate progress. If donating to a food pantry is your garden's mission, tell the group what you donated last year and plan with them a specific production and donation goal for the coming season. Posting your progress and celebrating your accomplishments along the way and at the completion of a project will motivate kids and bring them together in pursuit of a common goal.

## LEADERSHIP DEVELOPMENT

Taking on meaningful leadership roles can also provide motivation. For many young people, being trusted with a leadership role may be a new experience, and support and communication are crucial in helping them succeed. Clearly develop and outline expectations—timelines, responsibilities, and short- and long-term goals—to assist in achieving the desired outcome. Use SMART (specific, measurable, attainable, realistic, and timely) goals and set times to check in on youth-led projects. Many youth-development gardening programs offer positions of increasing authority for returning participants who show leadership, such as crew leader, apprentice, intern, or assistant grower. If your garden does not employ titles with specific responsibilities, give thought to increasing responsibility and support for kids when they demonstrate that they are ready for a more challenging role.

Community gardens have a great opportunity to advance youth leadership because there is never a lack of important work to do. If you are looking for ideas for your garden or would like to share your accomplishments with other community gardens, the American Community Gardening Association and Cornell University's Garden Mosaics Action Projects database (www.gardenmosaics.cornell.edu) can be a great resource. Teens themselves are an excellent resource for identifying interesting and unique projects and for leading project crews. Young people, working individually or in groups, can provide leadership in a number of areas:

- **Garden enhancement** can include art projects like murals, mosaics, garden bed design, or construction using natural building techniques.

- **Garden maintenance** leaders can take responsibility for a specific task, such as pruning, starting seeds, or turning the compost pile, or choose a section of the garden to maintain.

- **Garden tracking** tasks are a good fit for youth who are inclined toward writing or math. They can write a garden newsletter or track data on pounds harvested or volunteers in attendance.

- **Garden advocacy** appeals to kids with a penchant for public speaking or performance and can include recruiting volunteers, leading garden tours, planning celebrations, educating visitors, presenting community demonstrations, and attending conferences.

Involving youth adds great value to your community garden, whatever the scale of your project. Employing team-building exercises to connect kids with each other and with adults, collaborating on meaningful work, and providing leadership opportunities for youngsters can sustain their interest while bringing fresh ideas to your garden and its mission. Young people who feel connected and empowered have a greater investment in the garden and in their community and will ultimately serve as the best advocates for making community gardens purposeful, beautiful, and safe.

## CODY'S STORY

I started working for the Food Project almost two years ago. I knew right from the start that I had found my life's passion. My work with the Food Project was physically challenging, yet extremely rewarding. I learned for the first time what it was like to get rid of weeds in the field and how to harvest the crops that I worked so hard to take care of. Each week, I would get to work at hunger relief organizations, where I would see the food I grew go to people who needed it most. Farm work was not all that I learned. Through workshops given to us by interns, I received valuable information about social diversity and healthy food choices. These workshops fueled me with knowledge that drastically changed the way I looked at the food system. A year later, as an intern, I got the chance to teach other youth the skills and knowledge that I learned as a crew worker. By teaching, I became even more familiar with the subject matter. The Food Project has shown me where my true talent lies and how I will look at food in the future. I am now looking into agriculture as my future career.

*Cody Urban (back row, center) works as an intern for the Food Project in Boston (www.thefoodproject.org).*

## Entrepreneurship Training

Community gardens can connect communities and youth on a third level: as a training ground for economic development "from the ground up." Young people are exposed to a variety of entrepreneurial activities in their home communities—from the legitimate to the illicit—and are influenced by the images, messages, and ideas that businesses communicate. While garden leaders may be unclear whether or not young people are interested in getting their hands dirty in a vacant lot down the street, most can agree that earning money is of almost universal appeal.

Connecting teens to garden work can increase economic development, raise awareness between generations, and make a visible, aesthetic difference in the community. Entrepreneurial activities range from those of grassroots start-ups to projects sponsored by sophisticated organizations. Community gardens across the nation can illustrate the power of entrepreneurship to engage youth.

### GETTING STARTED

Conceiving an idea for your business that is exciting for participants and fills a need in the surrounding community is primary. Generally, business ideas initiated by youth and facilitated by garden leaders prove to be the most sustainable. Entrepreneurial endeavors often arise organically, from ideas discussed during marathon weeding sessions or brainstorming about what to do with excess (plants, compost, produce) in the garden. Garden leaders may assist in the development of the idea by discussing examples of garden-based businesses developed by teens or by facilitating field trips to organizations with similar programs. In addition to examining the garden's products, thinking about opportunities within the community is vital. What community needs aren't being met? Are there challenges in the community that young people can address in a unique way? Kids possess a wealth of information about their neighborhoods and will likely come up with a number of ideas. Distilling them into one viable business concept may be the biggest challenge.

## SUCCESS STORIES

Once an idea "sticks," the prospect of leading a cadre of youngsters through the (seemingly) interminable steps of starting the business can be daunting. Fortunately, those who have gone before have been kind enough to document their trials and successes and have provided a roadmap for the rest of us to follow.

A local library is a great place to start, as it is free and readily accessible in most communities. *I Said Yes! Real Life Stories of Students, Teachers and Leaders Saying Yes! to Youth Entrepreneurship in America's Schools*, by Julie Silard Kantor, is an inspirational book filled with stories of young entrepreneurs and the leaders who helped them realize their ambitions. For an in-depth how-to guide to business development, the National Foundation for Teaching Entrepreneurship has developed a curriculum complete with teacher's guide, workbooks, and text.

The internet is an invaluable tool for technologically savvy youth, who can find links to information on other garden-based youth businesses around the country, city-sponsored sites with advertising opportunities for youth business (For example, BizKid$ in Rochester, New York), and business tools on a site run entirely by young entrepreneurs (kids4kids.biz), as well as other sites essential for business research, accounting tools, and business-plan templates. (See bbg.org/cg for additional resources.)

Garden produce sales are the most straightforward of garden-based businesses and a good way to draw youth into the garden, like here at Green Youth Farm in Chicago.

## GARDEN PRODUCE SALES

Garden produce sales (including plants, produce, cut flowers, raw honey, eggs, etc.) are the most straightforward of garden-based businesses and are a good starting point for drawing youth into the garden. Farm stands and markets are not only a means to added profits for participants but also a venue for learning valuable customer-service skills, basic accounting, and salesmanship. Several venues for produce sales exist:

• **U-pick**—youth welcome members of the community to the garden to harvest in-season produce at a reduced price.

• **Weekly farm stands**—youth sell garden produce in or near their garden, not necessarily at a set time.

• **Farmers' markets**—youth sell garden produce at markets organized by a larger entity that are held at a set time and not necessarily in the community of the garden, often entailing a vendor fee.

• **Community supported agriculture (CSA)**—community members commit to buy a certain amount of produce on a regular basis and in exchange receive an assortment of whatever produce is ready for harvest throughout the growing season.

At Green Youth Farm, teens have gradually expanded their participation in produce sales from U-pick to a multifaceted approach that incorporates all of the venues mentioned above. The North Chicago/Waukegan site continues to hold a weekly U-pick market and offers a farm stand at the cultural center on site. Established farmers' markets organized by the Chicago Department of Special Events and by the USDA's Women, Infants and Children Program in Waukegan are also part of the weekly responsibilities for Green Youth Farm students. During the 2007 season, produce sales expanded to Saturday farmers' markets at the Chicago Botanic Garden and a small CSA serving Chicago Botanic Garden staff.

## VALUE-ADDED PRODUCT SALES

Value-added products—created when the producer increases the worth of the raw materials produced in the garden through a variety of means (including packaging, processing, cooking, crafting, etc.)—have the potential to help youth realize higher profits from their garden-based business. Producing them can be a great way to help engage youngsters during off-peak times when little or no work is required in the garden. Depending on the product they select to create and market, there is the potential for a much more significant investment of time, energy, and money than required for produce sales. The creation of even a basic business plan can help determine if the product selected will be feasible on a number of fronts. At a minimum, the group may wish to ask the following questions: Does a real market exist for your product? Do you have enough youth buy-in to sustain the sometimes tedious process of busi-

**Farm stands such as this one at Chicago's Green Youth Farm offer lessons in customer-service skills, basic accounting, and salesmanship.**

ness development? Are there opportunities within the business plan to incorporate new members and future development into the business?

## GARDEN SERVICES

The community garden is a great training ground for youth to learn the skills needed to begin a garden-based service business. Services such as snow shoveling, tool sharpening, leaf raking, compost turning, and weeding are often too time consuming and physically taxing for many community residents, making for high demand for these services and low supply of affordable providers who are willing to work on a small scale. Association with the community garden can give the young people employed by the business added legitimacy within the community and may help to strengthen generational ties. In addition to earning extra cash for the youth in the neighborhood, a garden-service business can teach them customer-service skills and life skills for when they own their own home in a community.

In neighborhoods across the country, garden-based youth programs are helping teens learn about food, leadership, and community. The programs help teens develop practical skills and can be catalysts for profound experiences. Perhaps most essentially, community gardens can inspire youth to cultivate ideas of value and a sense of what to do with their lives.

# Therapeutic Horticulture

## Susan Fields

In 1997 a weedy lot at Sixth Street Baptist Church in New Orleans was transformed into the God's Vineyard Community Garden—with the goal of growing food for the hungry while providing activities for senior citizens. But it was boys, ages 6 to 12 years, who came day after day to tend the garden. "We never recruited boys," recalls Noel Jones, one of the project's founders. "They just kept showing up." Most of the boys came from the same large housing project, but they represented different areas within the complex, and in the beginning there were fights. According to Jones, "We spent one hour breaking up fights, fifteen minutes gardening," until the garden adopted animals. Once the boys began caring for the chickens, ducks, and rabbits and growing vegetables, they set aside their differences. "It made something dependent on them—they had to be there to provide food and water. It was therapeutic to have something to grow, to nurture," says Jones.

## God's Vineyard Community Garden
### NEW ORLEANS, LOUISIANA

God's Vineyard grew with the needs of the young gardeners. Many would come straight from school and stay until the evening. Jones and the project's cofounder, Earl Antwine, began sending food home with boys for supper. Soon the children started identifying people in their community in need of food, and the small garden project evolved into a community food bank. By 2005, the food bank was serving 1,500 people each week.

Discussions during Saturday planning meetings with the youth revealed that many of them had unrealistic or hazy plans for the future. When the garden received a small business grant, the growers started an entrepreneurial project that could help raise funds for the young growers to go on to trade school or college. The resulting product, St. Thomas Seven Pepper Hot Sauce, taught the boys about seed selection, food preparation and preservation, marketing, and hard work. And as the boys began answering questions about their crops, animals, and product, Jones noticed their social skills and self-confidence increase. "The change may not be something you saw right away, but over time they became proud."

**James Kuhns, former president of the American Community Gardening Association, harvests tomatoes, beans, and parsley from a raised bed planter in Toronto's East York community garden.**

In 2005, Hurricane Katrina scattered the God's Vineyard growers across the country. Noel Jones worries about the 40 boys who once grew peppers for their hot sauce, but says, "One thing we tried to do was teach them they couldn't wait for someone else; they have to get out there and do something, do what is needed. They took a lot away from the experience."

## Healing Gardens

Many community gardens begin as healing projects—an individual, a neighborhood, or a society seeks to restore balance, ease suffering, heal wounds, create beauty out of chaos, nourish hunger, make a place for the forgotten, or inspire new generations. In the same way that the God's Vineyard garden project in New Orleans began as a hunger-relief and social program for seniors but rapidly evolved into a youth-development project, community gardens often provide multiple layers of positive benefit for participants and their surrounding communities.

Community gardens were key in healing the social fragmentation that ailed many North American urban areas in the 1970s. Today, city dwellers all over the world seek green refuges from long work hours, a hectic pace of life, and the noise pollution endemic to our crowded urban areas. And there is increasing attention within the health and human service fields to what most gardeners know intuitively—that time spent in the garden is restorative.

### WHY IS GARDENING THERAPEUTIC?

Anyone who has ever turned a compost pile on a warm spring day knows gardening provides a good workout. But the positive effects of gardening go beyond the benefits of regular exercise. Physical rehabilitation specialists know that carefully deadheading marigolds or dropping tiny lettuce seeds into seed-starting trays improves fine motor skills and eye-hand coordination, and that gripping a rake and leveling a garden bed strengthens gross motor skills. Therapists working with patients recovering from brain injuries use the scent of fresh herbs such as rosemary

**St. Thomas Seven Pepper Hot Sauce, a project of God's Vineyard in New Orleans, taught young gardeners entrepreneurial skills and increased their self-confidence.**

and lavender to stimulate the senses. And recreation counselors lead patients with Alzheimer's disease on walks through rose gardens to rekindle fading memories. According to the American Horticultural Therapy Association, studies show that additional cognitive, psychological, social, and physical benefits of nature include decreased anxiety and improvements in concentration, immune response, social integration, and group cohesiveness.

Texas A&M University professor Robert Ulrich found in a groundbreaking study published in 1984 that recovering surgical patients with a tree view had shorter postoperative stays, received fewer negative evaluations from attending nurses, used lower amounts of analgesic drugs, and had slightly fewer postsurgical complications. In subsequent research he has found that views of natural landscapes positively affect heart rate, brain waves, blood pressure, and muscle tension. Ulrich and others have suggested that these benefits often occur within minutes of viewing natural or landscaped areas. Ulrich theorizes that gardens improve health outcomes because of their ability to alleviate stress, increase a sense of control over one's environment, and provide healthful distraction.

Rachel Kaplan, at the University of Michigan, has conducted extensive research on the value of what she calls "nearby nature." She believes that contact with nature is an essential component of human well-being. Significantly, her research suggests that many of the positive benefits may be gained from even a passive view of natural elements such as a potted plant, a tree outside one's window, or a small garden patch. According to Kaplan, a short visit to gaze at a flower garden, an afternoon spent weeding a vegetable plot, or a few stolen moments tending an indoor tropical plant all have the ability to support the healing process.

One prominent theory about our preference for natural landscapes is that despite our relatively recent movement into built environments, we are still deeply influenced by our history in the wild. Research has shown that humans prefer landscapes resembling those of their earliest ancestors. As these anthropoid forebears moved down from the trees, current evidence suggests they moved into the African savanna, the landscape most consistently selected as a preferred environment by study participants. Charles Lewis, professional horticulturist and a pioneer in the field of horticultural therapy, described humans as being genetically hardwired to prefer natural landscapes because our ancestors' very survival depended on their environment. By living in increasingly developed, concrete habitats, humans may be out of sync with their genetic heritage.

Whether we are genetically imprinted to prefer natural environments or not, many people find the rhythms of nature to be a reassuring pulse by which to orient one's life. As ecologist Rachel Carson once said, "There is something infinitely healing in the repeated refrains of nature—the assurance that dawn comes after night, and spring after winter." Gardening requires one to step outside of one's busy life and notice the daily weather patterns and changing seasons. Horticultural activities restore personal contact with the natural world, thus soothing the tensions of modern life.

## Urban Oasis at Kingsboro Psychiatric Center
### BROOKLYN, NEW YORK

Urban Oasis began in 1997 with a few flats of flowers and vegetable starts sold to maintenance staff. Today, the horticultural therapy and vocational training program encompasses two greenhouses, a small urban farm, a farmers' market, indoor plant propagation, nature crafts, and landscaping services. Susan Braverman, a rehabilitation counselor and master horticultural therapist, founded the program to serve mental health care recipients at the Kingsboro Psychiatric Center, a New York State Office of Mental Health facility. Braverman is quick to credit the program's success to the support she has received from the institution's administration and fellow staff members, as well as from Cornell University Cooperative Extension, the Horticultural Society of New York City, Brooklyn Botanic Garden, and the New York State Department of Agriculture and Markets. She reserves her highest praise, however, for the program's participants: "What is most meaningful to me about Urban Oasis is the amazing group of clients I work with. They are my heroes, who teach me lessons in horticulture and life, making our program a bountiful Eden."

Participants in Urban Oasis receive practical training in horticulture and gain invaluable job-readiness skills that prepare them for future employment or education. While selling fresh vegetables and houseplants at the seasonal weekly farmers' market, clients are recognized for their hard work, growing expertise, and the quality of their product. In addition to enhancing their self-esteem and sense of pride, Braverman says, the market allows for more natural integration with the general public and "levels the playing field." Clients become experts on vegetables and have opportunities to teach shoppers and each other. This can be a rare experience for institutionalized patients, who often lose the sense of having control over their environment.

The emotional benefits reported by program participants include a reduction of stress and an alleviation of depression. "When I feel depressed I look at Mother Nature," says one gardener. "It gives you a sense of life. It makes it feel worth living." These growers also describe gaining cognitive benefits such as improved concentration, anger management, and problem-solving skills. Says another participant, "It helps me connect with reality. I can clearly see what I am doing. If I make a mistake I see it." And of course there is the lesson in delayed gratification that all gardeners learn anew each spring. Another important benefit conveyed by participants is the sense of a profound connection to nature and the cycles of life. Gardening also helps strengthen social ties and restore important emotional bonds when it is a shared activity.

The local community has benefited from having a farmers' market selling fresh fruits and vegetables, including varieties desired by the surrounding Caribbean pop-

**The emotional benefits reported by participants in the Urban Oasis horticultural therapy and vocational training program include a reduction of stress and an alleviation of depression.**

ulation, such as callaloo, bitter melon, okra, long beans, malabar spinach, eggplant, cucumbers, sweet and hot peppers, basil, thyme, and lemon balm. Each year, the program distributes over 250 flats of vegetable starts at no cost to dozens of community gardens through a contract with GreenThumb, the community gardening program of the New York City Parks and Recreation Department.

Perhaps the most significant community benefit is the development of trained, motivated individuals hopeful about their own futures and that of the greater environment. "By working at Urban Oasis I now have a vision for how the city should look," says one gardener. "More landscaping, more trees, more grass. I want the city to be greener."

## Sixth Judicial District Community Supervision and Correction Department of Lamar County
### PARIS, TEXAS

The horticultural therapy program of the Sixth Judicial District Community Supervision and Correction Department of Lamar County grew out of the charge given by state district judge Jim Lovett to find new ways to protect the public and secure full restitution while reducing the recidivism rate among probationers. With the assistance of Kansas State University's Dr. Richard Mattson, a recognized authority in the field of horticultural therapy, the department launched a pilot program in 1997. The horticulture program was designed to teach vocational and job-readiness skills, increase levels of community involvement, improve self-awareness, promote positive emotional growth, and decrease the number of probationers committing future crimes.

In Lamar County, Texas, a probationer in the Sixth Judicial District horticultural therapy group plants pansies as part of a community service program.

A four-phase study began in early 2001 to track the program's outcomes. Probationers assigned to the horticultural therapy group were compared with probationers assigned to more traditional community service programs, including trash pickup, cemetery maintenance, and janitorial work. Two years after completion of the study the program's results were impressive: Participants in the horticultural therapy program had a 74 percent nonrecidivism rate compared with 51 percent for participants in the traditional program. "Horticulture therapy has reduced recidivism by 23 percent," says Lovett. "If you projected that statewide, we could save about $88 million a year in prison costs." About 400 probationers involved in the initial research are being tracked over a ten-year period to provide data on long-term results.

A potting shed, greenhouse, and atrium, raised beds for vegetables and flowers, and an herb therapy garden are the sites of daily gardening activities. Probationers learn about starting plants from seed, propagating plants, cultivating soil, and creating compost. Jimmy Don Nicholson, director of the Community Service Restitution Program and a trained horticultural therapist, observes improvements almost immediately. "When they come for their first community service orientation, probationers come out of the hard concrete world of the cities and courts and enter into the world of the garden and greenhouse. We immediately begin to see a change of focus—they let their guard down and communicate better." Nicholson uses garden maintenance to help probationers start a process of reflecting on their lives and making positive changes. "I begin with the metaphor of weeding, showing them healthy plants that have been properly maintained versus a weedy bed of distressed plants, and I say, 'Some of you have so many weeds in your life that you can't be seen; you have bad habits and influences in your life that we need to weed out.' "

An indoor butterfly garden, a caterpillar house, and an outdoor learning center are recent amenities that allow probationers to improve their communication and social-interaction skills by working as docents during tours for local organizations. Schools, garden clubs, and community members visit the butterfly garden to be delighted and learn about the life cycles of local pollinators. All of the plant material used as host plants for the caterpillars and as nectar plants for the adult butterflies is propagated onsite.

Other ways that probationers reconnect with the community are by growing food for donation, beautifying county bridges through landscaping efforts, and facilitating community planting projects at local schools. Several community gardens have received probationer assistance with cleaning up vacant lots, removing debris, and cultivating soil. According to Nicholson, local residents often approach the probationers to thank them for their work improving the community—thus mitigating the feelings of alienation and isolation that can be common among probationers.

## Horticultural Therapy, an Emerging Profession

As far back as ancient Egypt, time spent in gardens has been prescribed for restoration of the body and spirit. And nearly two centuries ago the mental health benefits of gardening began to be recognized by the budding American medical establishment. In 1812, Dr. Benjamin Rush, a signer of the Declaration of Independence and one of the fathers of modern psychiatry, published a book that advised the use of agricultural activities in the treatment of mental illness. A few years later the first private psychiatric hospital, the Friends Asylum in Philadelphia, integrated vegetable and fruit growing and parklike settings into its programs. In 1919, the Menninger Foundation, specializing in mental health care, opened in Topeka, Kansas, and began using gardening and contact with the natural world as treatment modalities. During World War I, gardening activities were used in hospitals as recreation for wounded soldiers. By World War II, structured horticultural activities were used for rehabilitative purposes; garden clubs around the country became involved in supporting these programs in Veterans Affairs hospitals.

The term *horticultural therapy* was first coined in the 1940s, and Michigan State University awarded the first master of science degree in horticultural therapy in 1955. A significant step in the emergence of the new profession occurred in the early 1970s, when the Menninger Foundation joined with the horticulture department of Kansas State University to create a curriculum and degree program in horticultural therapy. A professional organization for horticultural therapists was founded in the 1970s and became known as the American Horticultural Therapy Association (AHTA) in 1988.

## TIPS FOR COMMUNITY GARDENS WORKING WITH HORTICULTURAL THERAPY PROGRAMS:

- Learn from horticultural therapy professionals how to design accessible gardens and make adaptive gardening tools.
- Host horticultural therapy programs from local health care facilities that do not have access to outdoor growing areas.
- Invite community service–focused programs to assist with heavy landscaping needs such as clearing vacant lots, tilling soil, or implementing large plantings.
- Introduce garden members to the profession of horticultural therapy.

## TIPS FOR HORTICULTURAL THERAPY PROGRAMS WORKING WITH COMMUNITY GARDENS:

- Organize and invite local garden groups to symposiums on accessible garden design, the healing effects of people-plant connections, and strategies for promoting wellness through gardening.
- Earn income by growing plant material (veggie starts, ornamentals, native plants) for community gardens to use in the garden or sell at plant sales.
- Grow organic fruits and vegetables to sell at garden-based farmers' markets or to donate to emergency food providers.

**At the Carrie McCracken (TRUCE) Garden in Manhattan, community gardeners pick up plants that were started from seed by Urban Oasis participants. Each year over 250 flats of veggie starts are distributed through a program facilitated by GreenThumb.**

Today, therapeutic horticulture programs are found in hospitals and other health care facilities, schools, correctional institutions, assisted-living and senior centers, vocational and rehabilitative programs, residential centers, and public gardens. As interest in the field has grown, efforts have been made to differentiate the types of programs associated with this profession. The practice of *horticultural therapy* is defined by AHTA thus:

> Horticultural therapy is the engagement of a client in horticultural activities facilitated by a trained therapist to achieve specific and documented treatment goals. AHTA believes that horticultural therapy is an active process which occurs in the context of an established treatment plan where the process itself is considered the therapeutic activity rather than the end product. Horticultural therapy programs can be found in a wide variety of healthcare, rehabilitative, and residential settings.

AHTA distinguishes *therapeutic horticulture* from horticultural therapy. The therapeutic horticulture program leader will have training in the use of horticulture as a medium for human well-being, but program goals are not clinically defined and documented as they are in horticultural therapy. *Social horticulture* or *community horticulture* describes gardening activities that do not involve explicit treatment goals or a trained therapist yet still promote many of the benefits discussed in this chapter. Many community gardening projects—like God's Vineyard in New Orleans—are examples of social or community horticulture. And many formal horticultural therapy programs have strong ties with community gardens.

## Bringing Therapeutic Horticulture Into the Community Garden

Community gardening and therapeutic horticulture are both rooted in the healing effects of people-plant interaction. Both types of programs attract individuals who care about their connection to the natural world. Both serve as training ground for people interested in the horticulture industry. Each allows empowering role reversals: By nurturing living plants, individuals and communities become care givers instead of care receivers. The design and creation of a space that is welcoming to people with diverse abilities is just as essential to the success of a neighborhood garden as to a therapeutic garden. And innovations in adapting garden tools for differing abilities will be increasingly welcomed in community gardens as the baby boomer generation ages.

Community gardens offer great locations for professional horticultural therapy programs, which are often sited at institutions that lack gardening facilities. Gardeners and horticultural therapy program participants can partner on many gardening tasks, from building sites to starting seeds to selling at market.

As the world's urban population centers become more crowded and social stressors increase, therapeutic horticulture becomes more important than ever. The good news is that more people are not only gaining awareness of the healing effects of gardening but becoming skilled in its therapeutic usage as well.

# Growing New Americans

## Aaron Reser

Even in the busiest metropolis, early mornings in the garden can be the most peaceful of times; fog lifts and the city begins to wake up, and those of us lucky enough to tromp through the dewy grass and brush our legs against damp eggplant leaves and squash vines find ourselves with a moment of pause before the day begins. Only when I arrived at the garden in the earliest of my early mornings would I sometimes catch a gray-haired woman stooped over a patch of vegetables. The gardener, one of many Hmong women who found her feet on the cold midwestern soil in the late 1990s, was a regular at a garden where I worked in St. Paul, Minnesota. How this woman learned about the garden is to this day a mystery to me, but I like to think that she wandered by on a walk or heard about it from a friend and was drawn to the welcoming space by a longing to put her hands to the soil. "One touch of nature makes the whole world kin," says Shakespeare.

She worked in a section of the garden open to anyone and would harvest small handfuls, flash a wrinkled grin at me, and race off before I could attempt any communication beyond a smile. It seemed that the garden was a space where we both were content. Though I know nothing of her story, in my mind she joins countless immigrants who have arrived in a new and daunting land and found community gardens to be a safe, open space that welcomes them into a world that is familiar. A little rich soil and a few seeds can produce a patch of home, and many a new face in North America has found a garden to offer a spot of fertile soil in which to put down their own roots and grow in a new community.

## Refugee Gardens

Community gardens often begin informally, built out of necessity. As spaces in flux they are a likely environment for absorbing new faces and supporting changing demographics. New Americans join community gardens for any number of reasons, some possibly unique to their past experiences. Community gardens can be remarkably transformative spaces and can offer healing environments for those coming from places of trauma.

**Kadija Hayir, the coordinator of the Somali Women's Community Garden at Lawrence Heights Community Centre in Toronto, holds freshly harvested swiss chard.**

## FROM GARDENS TO FARMS

A few immigrant farming projects exist in the U.S. to help community gardeners make a transition to larger scales of production, such as the National Immigrant Farming Initiative (immigrantfarming.org) and its New Farmer Development Project, which identifies, educates, and supports immigrants with agricultural experience by helping them become local farmers and establish small farms in the region.

Numerous refugee gardens exist in North America. In the 1990s, Hennepin County, home to the city of Minneapolis, saw the largest influx of refugees of any county in the U.S. Many gardens there are today tended by youth from Somalia, Ethiopia, and Sudan. Scars on many of the young hands working in the garden are visible testament to past experiences.

The Twin Cities have also absorbed high numbers of Asian refugees over the past two decades, providing opportunities for unique partnerships. The City of St. Paul and the nonprofit Farm in the City worked with a local organization, the Hmong American Partnership, to provide growing space in community gardens for Hmong refugees. So successful were their plots that eventually the Hmong gardeners grew enough to support a weekly farmers' market and a small produce subscription service. These people fled their homeland in Southeast Asia and suffered the loss of friends and family to enter a country unfamiliar and frequently unwelcoming. The garden provided them with community and an opportunity to relax into the rhythms of work in the soil, harvesting, and arranging flowers into bouquets for market.

Immigration into North America follows global politics, and as a result, in recent decades community gardens around the U.S. and Canada have seen a sharp increase in gardeners from strife-torn places like Somalia, Cambodia, and the Middle East. The Somali Bantu Farming Council of Colorado supports gardens in Denver that have become thriving spaces for displaced Somalians to pursue their cultural and agricultural traditions. The East Dallas Community Garden in Texas, started in the late 1980s as a project to assist Southeast Asian refugees, supports crops of water spinach, bitter melon, wax gourd, long beans, and taro. More recently the city of Boise, Idaho, has welcomed Iraqi refugees, who have found solace at the Refugee Community Garden at Ahavath Beth Israel synagogue, a four-acre garden tended by congregants also working in partnership with people coming from Somalia, Liberia, Afghanistan, Armenia, and Ukraine.

## Cultural Bridges

A garden can serve as a bridge to a community, not only as a place to physically work and socialize with other people but also as a stepping-stone toward finding paying work in the community. And the effects can be wide ranging. Articles in the American Community Gardening Association's annual publication *The Community Greening Review* often refer to the "multiplier effect" that community gardens can have in the arena of change. "As cultural differences fall away in the garden," one article notes, "neighbors join together to push for other community changes."

One vivid example is provided by the National Bitter Melon Council in Boston, an innovative project that through art and advocacy promotes bitter melon as a cultural bridge between disparate communities in a changing neighborhood. Bitter melon, a relative of the cucumber, is prized for its abundant vitamins and minerals as well as for its ability to help lower blood sugar levels and help control diabetes. It is cultivated in tropical regions of Latin America, the Caribbean, East Africa, and Asia but is a newcomer to North America—brought into community gardens by new Americans. In partnership with the Berkeley Street Community Gardens, local restaurants, and the Boston Center for the Arts, the council has sponsored public events and creative performances to promote the attitude that changes in the neighborhood's demographics are a positive cultural force.

## New Business

Social service organizations and government agencies often form partnerships to advocate for immigrant gardeners. For example, in 2004, in Sacramento, California, Opening Doors, Inc., a nonprofit organization providing financial-development services to immigrants, collaborated with the USDA Risk Management Agency and the Office of Refugee Resettlement to prepare for the arrival of 2,000 Hmong refugees. Priorities of the project included helping the refugees gain access to farm-

**A gardener harvests ho bah, Korean zucchini, in the Community Peace Garden in Minneapolis.**

land, markets, and knowledge of the regulatory environment for food crops. The project still works today to secure resources for area immigrant farmers.

For people struggling to find work and acceptance in a new place, community gardens can provide the very basic necessities of food and nourishment and can also offer a small sense of ownership and a way to make an income. Being able to provide for yourself and your family is a matter of pride and self-respect. Karen Washington, a longtime grower and active community gardener in New York City, says, "To grow your own food gives you a sort of power, and it gives you dignity." Washington has helped to create markets in the Bronx where local gardeners can profit from their plots. Similarly, the program East New York Farms! runs a weekly market in Brooklyn that allows local community gardeners, many from the Caribbean, to sell their vegetable surplus and value-added products every Saturday at a neighborhood market.

Eco-Vida, in Chicago, was founded by Neris Gonzales, an El Salvadoran ecologist who fled repression and torture in her home country. This urban ecology and farming project was started in Chicago's mostly Latino Pilsen neighborhood to encourage low-income residents, especially youth, to grow food for their own consumption and for profit. The project teaches that the food we eat represents the inextricable link between health of the human body and health of the environment. Eco-Vida, like many other urban gardening projects, found support from the organization Heifer International. Part of Heifer's backing came in the form of technical assistance with worm composting, and now Eco-Vida sells worm castings as fertilizer.

## Preserving Cultural Bonds

Community gardens can be a place to maintain and preserve old cultural ties in a world where everything else is new. In the noncompetitive, cooperative atmosphere of the garden, immigrant kids can feel comfortable speaking in English or in the language they grew up with. The Youth Farm and Market Project, in Minneapolis, runs a farming project for young people that embraces and celebrates the different backgrounds of their participants. Many of the young gardeners came from Mexico, Central America, and East Africa, and at Youth Farm, they are encouraged to share their knowledge and traditions with each other.

Ayan Hudle is a 14-year-old Youth Farm staff member whose family moved from Somalia to the U.S. in the late 1990s. She stresses the importance of teaching youth to make healthy food choices while passing on knowledge of her home country. "Here in the U.S., teens are faced with very bad food choices," she says. "At home we buy from a market with fresh food grown by someone you know, from your neighbor, or someone you have a relationship with. Youth Farm, here, shows kids where their food comes from." The gardens often feature plots dedicated to different continents, where kids can plant familiar foods from home and can learn about each

**Young gardeners in the Lyndale Neighborhood Program of the Youth Farm and Market Project in Minneapolis show off weeds.**

other's cultures. Community gardens can also provide a rare intergenerational space where unstructured time can be spent learning from older people. At Youth Farm, immigrant elders from the community are invited to participate and pass on their important horticultural—and cultural—knowledge to the kids.

Community gardens, after all, are about community, and about bridging differences. Tangible benefits abound: increased food resources, healthier citizens, more green spaces, and safer neighborhoods. New voices and new experiences bring with them new knowledge. (Never have I trellised so well as after observing my Hmong coworkers grow twice as many cucumbers as I thought possible!) From across the globe, gardeners bring with them deep histories of cultivation techniques, bountiful varieties of crops, and expansive culinary expertise. The very nature of gardening is about exchange and perpetuation. Just as the seeds we plant have been passed to us and we in turn pass along the seeds we grow, so it is with horticultural knowledge. And as seeds grow, so too the minds that are opened by diverse opinions and experiences.

# Pocket Parks and Small Community Gardens

## Daniel Winterbottom

Finding opportunities to garden and to preserve or create natural refuges within our growing cities requires more and more creativity. As many North American cities increase in density, available open spaces are being replaced by housing or commercial development. At the same time, many cities are expanding rapidly outward, without coordinated planning to integrate and preserve natural areas. Many neighborhoods are losing both wild and cultivated green spaces. In the face of these trends, such residual spaces as parking medians, traffic circles, utility and street rights-of-way, and odd-shaped lots offer untapped possibilities for gardening and the regreening of our urban communities.

When I work in cities and towns in Mexico and Guatemala, I am always struck by the variety of small spaces—courtyards, patios, balconies, alleys, and stairways—that are cleverly orchestrated into lush and colorful compact gardens. In the city of Antigua Guatemala, flowering plants, singing birds in cages, small water fountains, and decorative paving transform many small, central courtyards into verdant refuges, bringing nature into dwellings in a seamless transition from yard to house. Hanging pots overflowing with draping plants, bougainvillaea wrapping ornate columns and beams, and colorful containers with small trees and shrubs define and embellish the space and offer a sense of place. Although North America's climates, architecture, and cultures are very different from those of Guatemala, these models offer many inspiring points of departure to explore.

## Sites for Small Community Gardens

Mini-gardens can be created under electrical transmission lines, in linear parking strips, on unused street rights-of-way too steep for vehicle access, and on residual parcels converted into pocket parks.

### PARKING STRIPS AND TRAFFIC MEDIANS

Parking-strip and median gardens utilize the unpaved five- to six-foot-wide strips found between the street and the sidewalk in residential parts of a city. Most of these

**Chicago City Hall's rooftop demonstration garden offers habitat for local birds, bees, butterflies, and other beneficials and also supports research and educational outreach.**

strips are technically within the street right-of-way and are the property of the city. As neighbors develop these spaces, whole blocks can be transformed into linear gardens that offer pedestrians a wonderful experience as they navigate the city.

Paving can be used to facilitate access to parked cars; trees can be planted for shade as well as wildlife food and habitat; and perennials and shrubs can offer color and texture. Gardeners must consider water needs, as water sources may be scarce and irrigation lines will need to be fed beneath the sidewalk. Drought-tolerant plants are often used in these locations (check with your local native plant society, nature center, or botanic garden or arboretum for plant recommendations). Streetside garden maintenance chores such as hand watering and cultivation open up social opportunities with neighbors and other community members.

Medians between traffic lanes are similar to parking strips, though they are much less accessible. When planted, they provide a strong character for the community; some of the most famous are those with distinct trees that define a significant street within the neighborhood such as the live oaks of Esplanade Street near the French Quarter in New Orleans and Commonwealth Avenue in Boston with its giant American elms and their cousins, disease-resistant Japanese zelkovas. Plants with colorful foliage can also be used to create a memorable image. Retaining curbs or walls will absorb heat and dry out the soil, so choose tough plants for raised medians.

## STREET RIGHTS-OF-WAY

Some street rights-of-way are too steep for vehicle access or are otherwise unsuited for auto traffic and can be converted to gardens. These can be significant spaces, 50 to 60 feet wide and spanning one or more blocks. Terracing on steep grades uses retaining walls to create stepped, level areas for gardening. In Seattle, the Phinney Ridge community garden has converted a steep, unused street right-of-way into a

vegetable garden. Timber-retained beds are stacked up the slope, a small orchard has been restored, and paved social areas are situated among garden plots. Within the gardens, a pathway serves as a midblock connector that links neighbors and serves as an ad hoc community gathering space.

**Community gardeners transformed a median into a lush garden along Quesada Avenue in San Francisco.**

**Through the use of terraced beds a neglected street right-of-way in Seattle now serves as the vital and productive Phinney Ridge community garden.**

## NEW GARDEN SPACES

In some municipalities, formal procedures exist through which residents can apply to establish a garden. The city of Portland, Oregon, for example, has a program that supports the installation of traffic circles. Criteria for approval include documentation that a certain number of injuries to people have occurred over a defined period, neighborhood support for the installation, and community commitment to plant and maintain the circle.

Seattle's Heart of Phinney Park was once an awkward intersection, confusing for drivers and too expansive for safe pedestrian crossings. The community raised funds to convert it into a garden, and the city agreed to remove the street section and permit a small garden and gathering plaza. The plaza, ringed with seating and climbing stones, is surrounded by drifts of mixed perennial and shrub beds that continue down the street and serve as a garden gateway into the community. The informal plantings are drought tolerant and mostly native to the Northwest, and offer continuous seasonal interest to visitors as well as rich habitat for wildlife (see photo, page 81).

## ROOF GARDENS

Roof gardens utilize the abundance of flat roofs and terrace areas within cities to create gardens for food production, socializing, and beauty. A roof garden can also slow storm-water passage into municipal drain systems, capturing it instead to support plants. And recent surveys of established roof gardens in cities indicate that they can contribute to plant and animal diversity in urban areas.

The weight of soil, plants, and people can be substantial, however, and adequate structural support must be in place before a roof surface is considered for a garden.

**The roof of the Pete Gross House in Seattle is divided into three distinct spaces by different types of screens. The complexity helps make this small garden space feel much larger.**

Trees and heavier planters should be placed atop structural columns to support the load. Average soil is quite heavy when wet: about 70 pounds per cubic foot. Techniques to lighten growing media include mixing pumice or other lightweight materials into the soil. Drainage media such as polystyrene or plastic mats can be used in place of rock, and rooftop gardeners should use pots and planters made from durable plastic materials in lieu of terra-cotta or stone. Most roofs are very exposed to sun and wind, so desiccation is a concern. Plants must be carefully chosen and trees, arbors, or screens used to create shade and windbreaks.

The garden at the Schwab rehabilitation hospital in Chicago, which is used by patients who have suffered severe injuries often resulting in paralysis, offers a good example of a successful rooftop garden. Plantings include a waterfall garden, a meadow, a butterfly garden, and ornamental grasses and shade trees. A water feature and aromatic plantings stimulate the senses and allow users to engage with the plantings. Vine-covered arbors provide shade during the hot summers, and the gardens are linked by an Americans with Disabilities Act (ADA)–compliant path that incorporates elements used by the clients in their rehabilitation.

Roof gardeners have some specific challenges to consider:

- **Weight limits** Typically 50 pounds per square foot (this should be confirmed with a structural engineer prior to design)

- **Waterproofing**

- **Safety measures** Railings at all building edges, strong anchors and tie-downs to resist winds

- **Compliance with codes** Fire codes can stipulate 80 percent nonflammable materials and building codes requiring two means of egress
- **Appropriate plant selection** for shallow soil profiles (usually 12- to 24-inches deep) and desiccation caused by strong winds
- **Adequate lightweight drainage media** Often pumice or polystyrene pellets
- **Sources of water and electricity**

## SCHOOL GARDENS

School gardens, created as a component of an ecological learning program, often need stewardship when school is not in session. These gardens offer volunteers from the community the opportunity to garden during the summer months. School gardens range in size, and many use the smaller, residual spaces unoccupied by buildings, sports fields, and paths. They need the same creative planning and design that go into rooftop or parking-strip gardens.

Habitat gardens can be created on small plots at schools or other spaces such as public parks. Plants that provide shelter and food will attract butterflies, other insects, and birds, creating learning environments for human visitors. Many public and private civic organizations have significant parcels of land surrounding their buildings, and utilizing that land as gardens can strengthen community engagement, improve ecological functions, and beautify the grounds. Examples include gardens at libraries, churches, and on vacant lots, usually of an odd shape impractical for development.

# Strategies for Gardening in Small Spaces

The following considerations and strategies are important in any garden, but they are particularly useful when space is at a premium.

## VERTICAL GARDENS

Vertical gardens can work in spaces where planting beds are not feasible, such as small balconies, narrow alleyways, or tiny courtyards. Vertical gardening is an ancient practice commonly found around the world. In China, for example, trellis structures are used to increase space for food production. Many types of melons and squashes are cultivated on trellises, while sweet peas and nasturtiums create colorful, edible walls. Trellises can also be used to define garden rooms with green partitions.

Vertical gardens typically require a freestanding or wall-mounted structure to support climbing vines. Support structures create visual interest and can be designed to complement or extend the architecture of the building into the landscape. Powder-coated metal is a more expensive material than wood but requires less maintenance. Simple trellises can be placed in bins filled with soil and planted with annual vines such as black-eyed Susan vine or morning glories, or perennials like native honeysuckle (*Lonicera sempervirens*), native wisteria (*Wisteria frutescens*), or native passion-

# STARTING OUT

The following steps are useful when developing a small community garden.

**Determine who owns the property and acquire access.** Is it legal to develop a garden on the site? Laws change between municipalities so a call to a local planner and/or permit specialist in the building department should clarify if gardening is an accepted use on the property and if so what permits are required. Below-the-radar gardening can challenge restrictive policies or transform a vacant lot with an absentee owner. However, it is not unheard of for well-established and beloved community gardens to be bulldozed by developers because legal permissions weren't obtained. The resources expended to create a garden are significant, and if a legal mechanism exists that will support community gardeners, it should be pursued.

**Perform a comprehensive site analysis.** Do a vegetation inventory and analyze wind and sun conditions, water supply and drainage, and contextual issues such as noise, abutting uses, privacy needs of neighbors, views in and out, and circulation into and around the site. Have the soil tested to determine fertility and if toxins or contaminants are present. Most urban soils need significant amending or complete removal or remediation (see bbg.org/cg for a site analysis checklist).

**Determine your budget prior to design.** Funding sources are often local and can include city, county, or state grants; foundation or individual support; in-kind material or labor donations; support from conservation or small business groups or Rotary clubs; and of course bake sales, auctions, and door-to-door solicitations.

**Define your goals and start building community involvement.**
Once your analysis is completed, a conceptual design can be developed. A

participatory method of design will engage the community and encourage stewardship and ownership of the project. Invite community members to attend public meetings, where their needs, visions, and problems can be voiced. As the garden design evolves, it should be presented to the stakeholders for input, resulting in a final design that is responsive to the community's particular needs.

**Gardeners at Nuestras Raíces in Holyoke, Massachusetts, develop planting plans.**

flower species to form green, nearly opaque walls. Wall-mounted pots can turn a blank wall into a vertical container garden.

## RAIN GARDENS

Rain gardens are being used with increasing frequency by homeowners, businesses, and municipalities to catch rainwater flowing from impervious surfaces and prevent overtaxing storm drain systems. Rain gardens are created by directing storm water into planted swales, or depressions. To channel storm water on a curbed street, slots are cut into the curb, allowing water to flow through into the swale. Downspouts can be piped to swales to convey roof runoff into the rain garden.

**The rain garden at the Portland conference center uses local stone to convey rainwater from the roof scupper into an extensive swale system.**

Soils have differing moisture regimes, and plants that thrive in these various conditions must be carefully chosen for a rain garden. Gravity plays its part, too. Plants tolerant of the wettest conditions are planted at the lowest points; those that can sustain some moisture are used in the middle areas; and the least moisture tolerant plants are placed at the highest edges of the swale. Many municipalities publish recommendations for rain garden plants and describe how to build and maintain these gardens.

## DESIGNING FOR ACCESS

Designing for universal access offers a particular challenge in small garden spaces, especially those with significant grade changes. Accessible planters and activities should be placed as close to the entry as possible. Appropriate paving surfaces, raised beds, paths with adequate turning radii, and railings and grab bars will help people of differing abilities enjoy the garden.

## GARDEN ANIMALS

Animals can be incorporated into small gardens, though the size of the animals should be proportional to the garden. Rabbit hutches, chicken pens, and birdcages may be installed to introduce animals that require small amounts of space. Chickens can often be left to run inside the garden, providing natural insect control. Care should be taken to prevent attacks by dogs or cats; when animals are introduced into the garden, fencing should be employed to prevent the animals from leaving the garden and predators from entering.

The front yard garden at the author's house in Seattle extends into the parking strip, increasing the size of the garden and enhancing the experience for those using the sidewalk.

## DESIGN AND PLANT SELECTION

The design of a garden is often uniquely personalized, but following a structured process may be helpful. Spend as much time as possible on the site during different seasons and times of day. Try to get a sense of place and observe the way the site is currently used to better understand any inherent challenges. Learn what degree of maintenance will be provided and what resources are available. Simultaneously, develop the project goals and objectives, as these will become the guiding principles for the design.

I visit the site with a list of programmatic elements and visualize how they might fit on the site and best complement its attributes. Returning to the studio, I develop a series of drawings that diagram these elements. For example, if the chosen elements are gathering area, kids' play area, vegetable beds, outdoor classroom, composting area, and an orchard, I'll draw bubbles to the scale of the area needed for each to create diagrams that show the relationships between these elements. Once the program diagram is finalized, I develop the circulation patterns, locate service areas, and figure out what infrastructure (retaining walls, fences, drains, etc.) will be needed. The structures like arbors, fences, water features, walls, and accessories can then be located, followed by trees, shrubs, and perennials beds, then vines and annuals. Once the design is resolved, details are developed for the built elements and planting plans showing plant types, locations, and quantities are created.

## GETTING A SENSE OF PLACE

For a list of elements to survey before planning your garden design, visit **bbg.org/cg.**

Plant selection for a small garden offers many opportunities to express seasonality, color, texture, and fragrance and to cultivate food and herbs. Small trees may be a better choice than large ones so that the sun is not entirely blocked out; many dwarf cultivars of crabapple and small flowering ornamentals such as snowbell, lilac, and fruit trees are available. Beneath the trees, plant drifts of small shrubs or shorter ornamental grasses. Groundcovers can create textured carpets of foliage—often with colorful flowers too. Turf offers an inviting surface for sitting, but lawns are high-maintenance features and in a small garden should be used judiciously. Other plantings can create visual interest and create a depth of field, particularly important in a small space.

## Plant Selection Tips:

- **Arrange pots, planters, planting beds, screens, and walls to create complexity and expand the depth of field,** visually transforming a small garden into one that feels much larger than it really is.

- **Situate specimen plants, sculptures, and architectural features as focal points** within the garden that visually lead the user through the space.

- **Choose trees that are proportional to the size of the garden.** Smaller trees, possibly dwarf cultivars, will allow more sun into the site. A combination of deciduous and evergreen plantings will increase complexity and year-round interest.

- **Select plants that will provide seasonal interest** with their leaves, flowers, berries, and bark. Use annuals for color accents.

- **Hanging planters and climbing vines** can increase the quantity of vegetation and color while using a minimum amount of planting space.

- **Consider using steps and low walls for seating,** thereby reserving space for plants.

- **Modest water features** muffle surrounding noises, add visual interest, and relieve stress for users.

From lush gardens to compact vegetable plots, small-scale community gardens offer a variety of engagements, bringing together neighbors to participate in their creation, maintenance, and enjoyment. These compact urban oases beautify city streets and provide a sense of place. And you can always start small.

**Cast-off crutches form an innovative trellis for spaghetti squash at Riverdale Meadows community garden in Toronto.**

# Habitat Communities

## Pat and Clay Sutton

For those of us who live outside of urban centers, surrounded by green, it can be easy to take delight in our natural surroundings and forget just how disruptive human development is to wildlife habitat. Our yards and streets slice through wildlife corridors; nonnative plants escape out gardens and disrupt local ecosystems. To offset our impact on wildlife, it takes more than a patch of green on a single lot. Supporting habitat requires a different type of community gardening: a community of gardeners who work in concert across many pieces of land to provide food and shelter for pollinators and other wildlife.

## Building Community Support

As more and more backyard habitats and community habitat gardens are created, they collectively breathe life into the wildscape movement, encouraging it and connecting folks with like interests. Wildscaping is the process of making a garden more attractive to wildlife, often through offering native plants and various forms of shelter. Widespread community support is an essential ingredient, since habitat gardeners that do not have community support frequently come up against overzealous enforcement of weed laws. Wild Ones Natural Landscapers, an environmental advocacy nonprofit with chapters in a dozen states, shares extensive information on weed laws in the context of native plant landscaping and offers advice and ordinance models for encouraging the use of native plant communities as an alternative in urban landscape design.

Since habitat gardening is not yet the norm, educational signage often goes a long way to win over or at least appease a sometimes skeptical public. The National Wildlife Federation's "Certified Wildlife Habitat" sign and Monarch Watch's "Monarch Waystation" sign succinctly legitimize the wildlife garden and put its naturalistic, unmanicured plantings into perspective. Homemade signs can easily serve the same purpose. Visitors to habitat gardens can't help but notice the abundance of wildlife (butterflies, moths, dragonflies, bees, frogs, hummingbirds, and songbirds), and are often inspired to do something similar with their own yards. And if the visitor is a neighbor or lives in the same community, it usually isn't long before wildlife gardens are sprouting throughout town.

**Signs identify a habitat feature at the Magnuson Community Garden in Seattle.**

## Cape May, New Jersey

Every fall, birders and naturalists from all over the world make a pilgrimage to the tip of the Cape May Peninsula in New Jersey to witness the migration spectacle, involving millions of birds, monarch butterflies, dragonflies, and bats traveling from their summer breeding habitats to their overwintering grounds. More than 1,500 acres of wetland and upland habitats have been protected at the very tip of the peninsula, with additional lands protected just north of Cape May. But with millions of migrants passing through, this acreage is not enough. As elsewhere in North America, every square foot is of inestimable importance to hungry stopover migrants. So it's a boon to wildlife that the protected public areas are greatly augmented and complemented by a large number of back- and front-yard wildlife gardens as well as several community habitat gardens.

Our own habitat garden adventure began over 30 years ago when we purchased a half-acre property in a rural area located midway down the Cape May Peninsula. The home was old (dating to the 1830s), recently renovated, and charming. The yard, however, was bare. The previous owner shared that he had bulldozed everything except the back, where, thankfully for us, his equipment broke down. Today the back third of our property is a tiny bird-filled woodlot with a meandering mowed path, fondly called our "nature trail," passing through those native trees the bulldozer spared. Over time our woodlot of dwarf hackberries, American hollies, sassafras, sweet gums, black locusts, and red cedars has been complemented by gardens full of native wildflowers (like bee balm, ironweed, Joe-pye weed, cardinal flower, goldenrods, mountain mint, and in our ponds, pickerelweed), shrubs (beach plum, buttonbush, New Jersey tea, sweet pepperbush), vines (coral honeysuckle and trumpet creeper), grasses (little bluestem), and six different milkweeds for hungry caterpillars. Taken together these plants, all of them native to the area, make up a richly layered habitat that's a haven for many species of bees, butterflies, moths, and other insects; bats and other mammals; amphibians; and birds.

At Cape May, as in many areas around the country, the enthusiasm of individual wildlife gardeners has inspired the creation of communities of backyard habitats. Curious individuals intrigued by the abundance of birds, bees, and butterflies in a neighbor's garden set out to emulate nature in their own yards and the community at large, giving up tidy lawns to make room for happy jumbles of nectar-rich native wildflowers, seed-bearing grasses, fruit-bearing shrubs, and sheltering trees.

Community wildlife gardens are vivid testament to the enthusiasm of wildlife lovers everywhere. Pavilion Circle is one of several community habitat garden projects in Cape May. Created by the Cape May Point Taxpayers Association in 1993 with generous support from residents and a tree grant, Pavilion Circle was transformed from a barren area of sand and prickly pear cactus into a varied landscape featuring tree and shrub plantings that attract songbirds during spring and fall

**Community habitat projects and protected areas support the millions of monarch butterflies and other hungry creatures that each year migrate through Cape May, New Jersey.**

migration, as well as overwintering birds in the colder months and nesting birds in summer; flower- and herb-filled gardens for butterflies and their voracious caterpillar offspring; and scattered benches for human visitors of all ages. Pavilion Circle's pathway of brick pavers recognizes donors and shows the level of community support. In addition, "Bed Fellows" have adopted and maintain gardens in the circle so each is unique; while "Bed Warmers" help fund plantings and maintenance.

Pavilion Circle and many other habitat gardens are showcased during butterfly walks and monarch butterfly tagging demonstrations sponsored by the New Jersey Audubon Society. The society's model backyard habitat at the Cape May Bird Observatory in nearby Goshen, which is maintained by volunteers, serves as an outdoor classroom full of ideas for garden planners, complete with extensive butterfly and hummingbird gardens, a dragonfly pond, a meadow of wildflowers and grasses, islands of native shrubs, and surrounding thickets of native trees, shrubs, and vines.

## Rio Grande Valley, Texas

The Rio Grande Valley in southern Texas is another hotspot for bird and butterfly migrants that has been vastly improved by the efforts of habitat gardeners. Wildlife habitat corridors where native plants flourish, nine World Birding Center properties, the North American Butterfly Association's International Butterfly Park, and many other butterfly and wildlife gardens have been created. Wildlife is benefiting greatly, and more visitors than ever are coming to the area.

Community involvement has led to the creation of the "Birding & Butterfly Map of the Rio Grande Valley," which highlights 88 annotated sites in six counties, from

# LEARNING FROM PLANTS AND WILDLIFE

## Marilyn Smith

Adapted from the Brooklyn Botanic Garden All-Region Guide *Gardening With Children*

Creating a habitat demonstration garden is a great project for community gardens. Habitat gardens not only support beneficial wildlife but also offer fun ways to learn about ecosystems and the interdependence of plant and animal communities. Children in particular enjoy habitat gardening activities.

Many experts believe that the unending complexity of nature stimulates positive development in children. Yet children today in our society spend less than half the amount of time playing outdoors as their parents did at the same age. Demographic analysis indicates that a rapidly growing number of children no longer have regular opportunities for playtime in nature. With more than 80 percent of the U.S. population now living in suburban or urban areas, we're raising a whole generation that's far removed from the natural world and the processes that sustain us.

What better way to connect children with the natural world than through gardening? The experience of gardening—planting a seed; watching it grow; nurturing the plant by watering, weeding, and guarding against pests; and waiting for it to bear fruit—teaches children many valuable lessons they will carry with them throughout their adult lives.

### START A NATURE JOURNAL

Many kids find a journal or scrapbook a great gateway to investigating the natural world and keeping a record that can be referenced later. Your child and you may want to record many observations and activities.

**Nature's Lunchbox** Look closely at the activity going on in the garden to gather clues about what animals eat and how they find nourishment for themselves and their families. Try to draw pictures of the plant parts that are commonly eaten. Are there enough plants for animals and people to share?

**Pollinators in the Garden** Most plants make seeds only after being pollinated by insects and other animals. Pollinators like butterflies and bees transfer pollen from the anther of one flower to the stigma of another. Different plants are attractive to different animals. Butterflies visit red, orange, yellow, pink, and blue flowers that offer a flat surface to land upon, such as clusters of flowers or broad petals. Bees go for yellow, blue, and purple flowers. Find a quiet spot near flowers where you can sit and observe what creatures come to visit. What pollinators do you see? What are the colors and shapes of the flowers being visited? What do they smell like?

A goldfinch feasts on purple coneflower seeds in a Cape May, New Jersey, community garden.

Seed Hunt It's not enough for a plant to make seeds; it must also find a way to move them where they have enough space and water to grow. Some seeds are lightweight and travel by wind. Other seeds travel by floating in water. However, many plants use animals to move their seeds around. They usually do this in one of three ways. Some plants have little dry fruits that stick to an animal's fur. Many plants make yummy fruits that animals love to eat. The seeds inside the fruit are often not digested, but pass through the animal unharmed, and come out the other end. Some animals, like squirrels, bury and store nuts and other fruits, and those left behind will have a chance to germinate.

Take a walk through the garden and see how many different seeds you can find. The best time to do this is in summer or early fall. Organize and separate your collection by size, shape, or color. How do you think each seed was able to move around? Use a field guide to identify the seeds or ask gardeners for help.

Nighttime Safari Plan a nighttime safari to explore the garden. You might want to choose an evening with a full moon to help you see better. Make a list of the things you find. What differences do you notice between your nighttime and daytime observations? Do you hear any sounds that are different from those you hear during the day?

## TIPS FOR ADULT CAREGIVERS

Use all your senses. Listen, smell, and watch with your child. Let your child experience the natural world with all her senses. Explain when it is okay to touch or taste and when to check with an adult first.

Be still. Observing nature may require sitting quietly for an extended period of time. This does not come easily to everyone. Work with your child, modeling the behavior and showing that being quiet offers its rewards and brings out the critters.

Get dirty. Gardening activities and nature explorations require hands-on interactions with soil, plants, and water—some of which invariably end up on hands, clothing, and shoes. Make sure all gardeners and explorers wear comfortable clothes that are up to the task. And don't be afraid to get dirty!

Padre Island on the Gulf of Mexico west to Zapata on the Rio Grande, and an additional eight sites in Mexico, just across the river. Flourishing butterfly gardens have been planted at many of the sites, using plants native to the immediate area. Some of the 88 sites are federal and state lands, others are county lands, and quite a few are municipal and community lands. Many schools have butterfly gardens that are planted and maintained by students and used to support the curriculum.

As for the birds and butterflies, what once were scattered oases are slowly being linked together to form the beginnings of a planned wildlife corridor that will one day link borderland wildscapes. The benefits to wildlife—and to the entire Rio Grande Valley community—are enormous. In part due to its subtropical climate and location but mainly because of community involvement and effort, the Rio Grande Valley has become perhaps the most popular destination for butterfly watchers in all of North America, and the local economy has received a nice boost. The populations of many butterfly species are expanding thanks to increased plantings of native caterpillar food plants and nectar plants.

## Inviting Wildlife Into Your Own Community

It's surprisingly easy to create an environment that's welcoming to bees, butterflies, moths, and other beneficial insects as well as birds and other critters that live in your community. With a few changes your community garden—and the surrounding neighborhood—can provide the four basic requirements that wildlife need to survive: food, water, shelter, and places to raise their offspring. The animals in turn will help out by pollinating flowers and vegetables and devouring destructive insect pests.

Once you're hooked on habitats, search for helpful regional information including lists of plants native to your area that are most beneficial to wildlife: those that provide food for birds, nectar for butterflies, moths, and other important pollinators, and those that are needed for egg laying by butterflies and moths. Regional information is not always easy to find. Contact local nature centers, botanic gardens, arboreta, and native plant societies. Often these organizations will also help you identify sources for free or low-cost seeds, seedlings, and saplings.

**Invite butterflies to your neighborhood.** Once armed with lists of your area's best nectar and caterpillar food plants, choose wisely. Find a sunny spot (or spots) for your butterfly garden and plant a shrub from your list as the garden's cornerstone with flower beds branching off from it. In the beds plant groupings of at least three to five

## NORTH AMERICAN BUTTERFLY ASSOCIATION

For area-specific gardening advice, NABA offers 40 regional brochures and has 33 chapters that can connect you with local habitat gardeners; see www.naba.org. For an extensive list of other habitat gardening resources, see bbg.org/cg.

perennials, three of each, to create massed plantings. Be sure to save a patch for a massed planting of annuals like zinnias, which bloom nonstop until the frost and are irresistible to butterflies. Don't forget to integrate caterpillar plants, like milkweeds and many herbs. The charm of butterflies flitting around a garden makes these beautiful pollinators the perfect goodwill ambassadors for a budding neighborhood habitat project.

**Lure natural predators.** Beneficial insects like ladybugs, lacewings, and parasitic wasps as well as spiders and harvestmen will also be attracted to these gardens, so…

**A birdbath in Heart of Phinney garden in Seattle provides water for local wildlife.**

**Don't use pesticides.** In a healthy garden of native plants, nature will take care of insect pests—beneficial insects will eat or parasitize insect pests. If you do use pesticides, you're likely to harm the very insects you've attracted, plus some of the residues inevitably find their way into nearby vegetable gardens or get washed out of the soil when it rains, eventually polluting local aquifers.

**Add a few layers.** Birds and other small animals seek places to avoid predators and weather and to nest in. Plantings that emulate the vertical layers of a natural woodland habitat will attract them. If there's already a nice shade tree nearby, consider adding a few layers to create an animal-friendly understory. For example, plant a few native fruit-bearing shrubs nearby. Add a native vine or two. Surround the lot with native herbaceous plants and grasses. Then place a bench for visitors to enjoy the shade and observe the wildlife in action. Be sure to choose locally native shrubs, vines, perennials, and grasses to lure wildlife into your garden. Natives are best suited to meet the needs of local wildlife because both have evolved together over millennia, forming mutually beneficial associations in the process.

**Provide water for wildlife throughout the year.** Set out one or several birdbaths, and keep them clean and filled year-round if possible. A mister, which can easily be attached to a hose using a "Y" connector, might attract bathing hummingbirds, songbirds, and migrant warblers spring through fall. Have it serve a dual purpose— plant nectar plants that like "wet feet" under it.

**Go easy on fall cleanup.** Don't cut back perennial plants and grasses until early spring. Leave seedpods to provide food for overwintering birds, and let leaf litter remain to provide winter homes for butterflies and other insects.

# Making Gardens Sustainable

## Lenny Librizzi

Sustainable is a term much in vogue these days, perhaps even in danger of wearing a little thin. But given that plants are adapted to perpetuate themselves, the concept of sustainability is at the very heart of horticulture: In the garden we can extract value from our plants without using up the garden's value for future visitors. Sustainable literally means "capable of being maintained." In the garden this means employing good cultural practices that support a system where the inputs necessary to grow plants—soil, seeds, water, nutrients, and labor—can be preserved and replenished.

A community garden additionally offers a model for many broader aspects of urban sustainability. Community gardeners have been growing their own organic food for many years and are now an important part of the movement toward locally produced food. They have been able to drastically reduce their food miles (the energy consumed in transporting food from farm to table), considering that much of the food the average American eats may have traveled 1,500 miles or more before it lands on the dinner table. Community gardeners also help to reduce waste through composting and recycling materials and supplies. They collect rainwater and practice other water-conservation techniques. Some are experimenting with using renewable energy sources in their gardens. Many are helping promote biodiversity by saving seeds and by creating habitat for insects and birds. Possibly most important, community gardeners are showing how groups of people can live and work together to accomplish all of these things.

A community garden may be used to raise food, as a decorative garden, or as an educational or rehabilitative facility, but whatever its goals, the creation and nurturing of community remains its central mission.

## Preserving Gardens as Communities

The demands involved in establishing and maintaining a small space where people work in close proximity and together make decisions on a number of issues can be quite challenging. Planning strategies for social and political sustainability is an important task that sometimes community gardeners forget to tackle.

**A simple path made of reclaimed material wends through the Strathcona Community Allotment Garden in Vancouver, British Columbia.**

## ORGANIZATION AND GOVERNANCE MODELS

The biggest difference between a community garden and a farm or backyard garden is how decisions are made. The farmer or homeowner alone decides what to plant and where, and when and how to water, weed, and harvest. In a community garden these decisions, and others, are made by the group. How a garden is governed—democratically, by consensus, by benevolent or harsh dictatorship, or through anarchy—can support the long-term survival of a garden or promote its early demise.

There are many models of governance. The Hattie Carthan Garden in Brooklyn is a large garden by New York City standards, with over 20,000 square feet of land and 30 plots gardened by about the same number of members. Once a year there is a mandatory meeting of members at which a president and other officers are elected, any available plots are assigned, and plans are made for the season. Most of the rest of the decisions during the year are made by the president. This form of delegated leadership seems to work well for this garden.

In other gardens, members meet more frequently and make decisions by consensus. Not everyone may agree on every decision but through group discussions an idea or suggestion might be amended until everyone is comfortable with going forward. It often takes longer for decisions to be reached, which may be frustrating to some members, and may even mean that some decisions are never made. The important point of a consensus process is that everyone who wishes to can have input in the decision.

In some community gardens, one person makes all of the decisions. This person may get this power because no one else wants it or because he or she takes control and doesn't allow others to participate. Although not ideal, this type of governance may work for a while—but it is not sustainable. If the controlling leader leaves no one is in charge, and if no other members have had the opportunity to develop leadership experience the garden may not survive.

## GARDEN RULES

For gardens to be sustainable as communities they must adopt rules or bylaws. Garden rules are important to ensure that everyone is treated equally and to help settle disputes. They can cover anything from basic goals like practicing safety and respecting your neighbor to more practical details on how plots are assigned, leaders chosen, or tasks distributed.

Many municipalities impose rules that apply to all community gardens, which can be used as a garden's guidelines. This may be helpful when individuals feel that a garden's rules are unfair or harsh; if the rules are citywide, they usually are practicable.

## PLAYING BY THE RULES

For links to examples of garden rules that, with a little adaptation, can serve the needs of most groups, visit **bbg.org/cg**.

# SITE PROTECTION

There can be no talk of sustainability unless the garden site is protected from development. Even if the land is not protected from the beginning, working toward permanence of both the site and the community garden group are part of the process of moving toward sustainability. By getting involved in community councils or community planning boards and forming coalitions, gardeners have worked to gain political power and to preserve their community gardens—often in the face of intense pressure from other interests. Here are some great precedents for community gardeners to use to make the case for land permanence:

A few municipalities have **community garden policies,** which codify the rights and responsibilities of both the municipality and the community gardeners. The policies can include details about user agreements and services provided by the city. Chicago created a comprehensive community garden policy in 1996 when the City of Chicago, Chicago Park District, and Forest Preserve District of Cook County joined forces to form NeighborSpace. The mission of this nonprofit group is to work with communities to identify, acquire, and ensure survival of permanent spaces that can be used as community gardens and parks, particularly in neighborhoods that have a low ratio of open space to population. The three governmental agencies also support NeighborSpace financially.

In Boston, the **city zoning regulations** include "Community Garden Open Space Subdistricts," a zoning category for "land appropriate for and limited to the cultivation of herbs, fruits, flowers, or vegetables." While this category may not ensure permanence, having community gardens listed as an option in the realm of land-use planning paves the way for discussions about permanency.

**Community garden land trusts** have been created in a number of cities. According to the Land Trust Alliance, a land trust is a nonprofit organization that as all or part of its mission actively works to conserve land by undertaking or assisting in land or conservation easement acquisition, or by its stewardship of such land or easements. The Madison (Wisconsin) Area Community Land Trust is an example of a 25-acre single-site land trust called Troy Gardens. The South End Lower Roxbury Open Space Land Trust, founded in 1991, permanently protects and manages 15 community gardens and pocket parks in Boston. In Providence, Southside Community Land Trust, founded in 1981, has preserved 5 acres of community gardens. The Neighborhood Gardens Association/A Philadelphia Land Trust, incorporated in 1986, holds title to 24 gardens.

In some cities community gardens are **classified as parkland.** Either the local parks department manages a community garden program (as in San Francisco and Portland, Oregon), allows gardens on parkland (as in Dayton, Ohio, and St. Paul, Minnesota), or the city protects community gardens as parkland (as in New York City and Seattle). Most often parkland is preserved as permanent open space, though there are some exceptions. Having a community garden on parkland probably means the garden will be permanent but does not guarantee it.

**Fences can be inviting while affording some security, such as the delightful fence designed by Julie Dermansky for the El Sol Brillante garden in Manhattan.**

## UMBRELLA AND SUPPORT GROUPS

Since most gardens are created and maintained by volunteers, many cities have support organizations of one type or another to assist with advice and services. These organizations often supply political connections, municipal information, or garden materials, and can help with programming, group dynamics, and garden preservation. They also organize workshops, small and large conferences, and events of all kinds to support community gardeners. This support can come from small, all-volunteer non-profit groups or larger local, regional, or national organizations like the American Community Garden Association (ACGA). Cooperative extension services, botanic gardens, public-private partnerships, and city agencies can also provide services to community gardeners (see Resources, page 110).

## PUBLIC RELATIONS

In order for a community garden to survive, it must have support not only from members but also from the community outside the garden gates. When a community garden is an active part of a neighborhood's social fabric and neighbors are aware of the garden's myriad benefits, the community will help sustain the garden over time. See "Bringing Community Into the Garden," page 100, for some specific strategies.

## Sustainable Design Elements

While the importance of the social and political issues that affect sustainability of community gardens cannot be overstated, most people start or join a community garden simply because they want to garden, to connect to the land in locations that are often dominated by concrete, steel, and glass. There are many ways to create a physically sustainable garden that preserves and replenishes natural resources. How a garden is designed and the materials and practices that are being used all play a role. The goals are to use renewable or repurposed material as much as possible, produce little or no waste, and minimize the use of outside inputs like electricity and water. Horticulture can be made sustainable by composting, seed saving, using plants that provide habitat for birds and beneficial insects, and employing low-input management techniques for weed and insect problems.

If you are developing a new project, you can design your garden space in such a way as to foster community and make the garden physically sustainable. Some key elements are a suitable fence, a welcoming entry, and inviting common areas. Found, reused, recycled, or scrap material from the site itself, a nearby construction project, or a material-matching service offer ways to avoid consuming new material—and the energy costs involved in its manufacture and transportation.

## FENCES, ENTRY AREAS, COMMON SPACES

"Good fences make good neighbors" is an old adage that is especially important in community gardens. In some city gardens, little or no fencing is wanted or needed; other sites require tall, secure fencing. Sometimes gardens are designed so that some areas are open and other areas fenced. Several gardens in Philadelphia leave areas close to the street open, with raised planters and benches, and fence in the rest of the site. This technique gives the gardeners some protection for their plants and vegetables and also provides passersby with access to plantings. Little or no fencing in Mr. McGregor's Garden in Dayton, Ohio, is appropriate for that location, where vandalism is not an issue. Many children garden there, and the low fencing helps support the child-friendly nature of the garden.

The Yesler Terrace garden, on housing authority property in Seattle, has dressed up its chain-link fence with bamboo, a sustainable product that also evokes home for the site's Southeast Asian gardeners. In other places, where more substantial fencing is required, wrought iron can be used. At the Joseph Daniel Wilson Memorial Garden in Manhattan, an artist fashioned a fence from steel plates left over from a metal-stamping process. The holes in the plates form interesting shapes, the steel is secure, and the material was reused locally instead of being shipped away and remilled. Steel and other kinds of substantial fencing give a sense of permanence to a garden space that less secure fencing might not.

There are several things you can do to make your garden entrance inviting and comfortable and encourage interaction and a sense of community. A small patio or plaza-type space with seating welcomes gardeners and visitors. Additional seating can be dispersed throughout the garden if the space is large or confined to a space under a tree or shade structure in a smaller garden. (If you are planting trees to pro-

# RAINWATER HARVESTING

There is something that community gardeners can do to minimize their water use while keeping a supply of water in their gardens: rainwater harvesting (RWH). This ancient practice of capturing water in tanks or cisterns for later use is widespread in Caribbean countries and in many African and Asian countries. Its use in urban areas in the United States and Canada is relatively recent, but a number of cities in both countries now have rain-barrel and downspout-disconnect programs. Community gardens in more than 20 cities, including Seattle, New York, Chicago, and Vancouver, are using RWH systems to provide water for irrigation.

One of the first community garden RWH systems, at the University Heights P-Patch in Seattle, was built in 2002 by gardeners and students from the University of Washington's Departments of Landscape Architecture, Industrial Design, and Art. At the same time in New York City, the Water Resources Group, a collaborative of city agencies and nonprofits, installed a system at the 1100 Block Bergen Street garden in Brooklyn. Droughts on both coasts the previous summer were the impetus for these parallel efforts.

The systems are very different because the distinct rainfall patterns in Seattle and New York required different solutions. Both cities receive between 40 and 50 inches of rain in a normal rainfall year, but Seattle gets most of its precipitation as light rain in the winter, when it is not needed, while New York's rainfall is spread throughout

the year, with as much rain in August as in March, but with dry spells between downpours. In Seattle, RWH systems are designed with a large capacity—usually 10,000 gallons or more—to capture as much rain as possible in winter to save for summer use. New York RWH systems are much smaller—usually 1,000 gallons or less—and are designed only for use during frost-free months.

**This fanciful rainwater cistern captures 3,800 gallons of water, which is used to irrigate the Garden of Eatin' in Seattle.**

vide shade, they should be planted where they don't block the sun for vegetables or other sun-loving plants. Consider the mature height and canopy spread when choosing a tree species or cultivar.)

An interesting idea for a shade structure or shed roofing is to use recycled cans or plastic containers. By cutting cylindrical containers lengthwise and connecting them in a wave or corrugated profile, a roof can be fashioned, as has been done at the Lower East Side Ecology Center's garden in Manhattan (see this roof at www.evpcnyc.org/leseco).

When urban community gardeners dig out plots, they often unearth old bricks from a building that once stood on the site. All sizes and shapes of brick or stone are useful to compose pathways or fill an allotted space. Interesting circular or other decorative patterns can be made using smaller, odd-shaped pieces. Even glass bottles can be sunk into the ground bottom up to make a patio or pathway more colorful. Attractive design elements not only make the garden enticing but also beautify the neighborhood—which helps to build support from the community.

**Bottle bottoms and other found materials form colorful mosaics at the Dias y Flores community garden in Manhattan.**

## SHEDS

Gardening can be hard work. Anything that helps to make the gardener's job easier will go a long way toward making a community garden sustainable. Tools and supplies are necessary for all aspects of growing plants, and having a secure place to store these items is important. Sometimes a storage place in an adjacent building is available, but in most cases some kind of shed in the garden is the best solution.

Sheds usually are made of wood, plastic, or steel. Another good, low-cost material is cob. The word *cob* comes from an Old English word meaning "lump or rounded mass." It is a mixture of clay, sand, straw, and water that is formed into the desired shapes. Examples of cob sheds can be found at City Farmer's Demonstration Garden at Kitsilano in Vancouver, British Columbia, and at the Karl Linn Garden in San Francisco. Cob building projects are inexpensive but very labor intensive—they could be great for building community while making a community building.

## ELECTRICITY

For most community gardens, electricity is just not available. Simple solar-powered lights to line pathways can be purchased at most hardware and home improvement stores and are easy to install. One way to get electricity when it is needed for the garden is by capturing sunlight using photovoltaic solar panels. One garden in Manhattan, the 6BC Botanical Garden, has installed solar panels on a shed and an arbor. The electricity generated is used for lights and to power a circulating pump for the garden's water feature. Batteries store the electricity for use on cloudy days.

This type of technology may be beyond the ability of the average community gardener, but often there is one gardener—or a friend or relative—who has the skills to set up such a system. The parts and materials needed are becoming more available and costs are coming down as more solar panels and other components are being manufactured. Often grants are available to community gardens to pay some or all of the cost of materials.

## WATER

Many community gardens struggle for access to water. In some cities, community gardens are billed for water like any other water customer. In other cities gardeners are allowed to use water from fire hydrants. The luckiest have water piped into the garden and don't pay a fee. Less fortunate gardeners resort to hauling containers of water from wherever it is available.

Water conservation is a key strategy for sustainability. Selecting drought-tolerant species, adding compost to soil to improve its water-holding capacity, using mulch to keep the soil from drying out, watering only in the early morning or early evening to keep the moisture from evaporating before it has a chance to reach plant roots, and using drip-irrigation systems to target watering to the root zone are all techniques that help minimize water use. But there are times when it doesn't pay to be stingy with water. Vegetable growers need to water, especially when starting seeds or transplanting seedlings. Vegetable plants that are stressed from lack of water will be more susceptible to pests and diseases and less productive than well-watered plants.

## SOIL AND COMPOST

Along with water, soil is the most valuable resource for a community gardener. Regardless of what type of soil is in the garden, making and adding compost is key to its health, fertility, and productivity. Compost adds organic material, moisture-holding capacity, and nutrients and helps balance soil pH.

Organic materials such as grass, leaves, and vegetable waste will eventually decay and form humus if left alone, but composting that is tightly managed by including the right proportion of carbon-rich and nitrogen-rich materials, air, and moisture produces humus that is ready to use in as little as six weeks, including curing time. Some gardens accept yard waste from their neighbors, coffee grounds from coffee shops, and vegetable waste from local farmers' markets. This type of waste management has the triple benefit of keeping material out of landfills or incinerators, making the garden a good neighbor, and creating an essential resource for gardeners.

Composting is a vital activity for sustaining any community garden. It can be labor intensive and is best managed by a dedicated person or committee. For more information on composting, contact your local sanitation or parks department, cooperative extension service, or botanic garden. Some even offer free compost.

## FOSTERING HABITAT FOR BIRDS AND BENEFICIAL INSECTS

Community gardeners using compost instead of commercial fertilizer are taking the first step toward ensuring biodiversity in the garden. A healthy soil makes healthy plants, minimizing pest problems and the need for pesticides. Creating habitat that attracts beneficial insects and birds further helps to control pests and encourage native pollinators.

Build nest boxes and plant regionally native trees and shrubs like junipers, cedars, dogwoods, and sassafras that provide nesting spots and fruit that birds enjoy. Flowering annuals and perennials like asters, cosmos, bee balm, and purple coneflower provide seeds attractive to birds that will also eat insect pests. For more information on gardens as habitat, see page 74.

## SEED SAVING

Many small, local seed companies are either going out of business or getting bought out by large corporations. Locally adapted plant varieties are being lost, as is the

**Solar panels at 6BC Botanical Garden in Manhattan collect renewable energy to power lights, small DC-run appliances, and a recirculating waterfall.**

genetic material needed to maintain biodiversity. By saving seeds, community gardeners can help keep plant varieties from becoming extinct.

There are a few rules and techniques that are important to remember about saving seeds. Only seeds from open-pollinated, not hybrid, plants should be saved. Open-pollinated plant seeds will produce new plants like the parent plants. Seeds from hybrid plants may be sterile or could produce plants like either parent or even another cultivar that was used to create the hybrid. Make sure harvested seeds are fully mature and are thoroughly dry before storing them. Store fully dried seeds in airtight, labeled containers in a cool, dry place.

The most important thing that community gardener seed savers can do is to share or swap seeds with others to increase plants' chances of survival. Community programs like Project Grow in Ann Arbor and the Food Not Lawns Seed Swap in Eugene, Oregon, sponsor seed swaps (see bbg.org/cg for a list of programs).

## Troubleshooting

### WEEDS

For the sustainable gardener, controlling weeds without resorting to chemicals is a challenge. The first step in minimizing weeds is mulching. The two to four inches of mulch used to hold moisture in the soil and moderate soil temperature can keep many weed seeds from germinating. Weeding can be a thankless job, but if done properly—before weeds get established—it will take less time and be more effective. Be sure to pull the roots in order to keep the weeds from resprouting. And make sure you can distinguish weed seedlings from your garden plants so you don't accidentally pull out the wrong ones.

In the vegetable garden, companion planting or interplanting plants such as carrots, onions, or garlic that utilize lots of root space with plants like lettuce and tomatoes that instead utilize lots of aboveground space creates a dense bed that will crowd out weeds or stop them from sprouting in the first place. Early intervention, crowding out weeds, or depriving them of sunlight make this aspect of sustainable gardening less onerous and help avoid the use of herbicides.

### RATS AND OTHER PESTS

According to some estimates, in some cities the rat population outnumbers the human population. A garden is a natural nesting area, so the key is to limit the availability of food, water, and places for rats to burrow. Avoid having open containers for water and food waste. Trash bags containing food waste or packaging, food left out for birds, and table scraps on compost heaps are all potential meals for rats. Keep trash in a closed container that is emptied regularly and work with residents of adjacent properties to do the same. In the compost area keep food waste in closed bins and turn open piles regularly to avoid creating nesting spots. In extreme cases rat baiting may be necessary. Make sure to follow the manufacturer's instructions and place the bait away from areas where other wildlife, pets, or humans may come in contact with it.

Squirrels may also be pests and can easily ruin a bulb garden in less time than it took to do the planting. If squirrels are a problem, bulbs or other new transplants may have to be protected with mesh screening until the plants become established. Or plant daffodils only; squirrels and other marauding wildlife will avoid eating their toxic leaves and bulbs.

**A sign proclaims this garden pesticide free, sending a healthy message to the community at large.**

## THEFT AND VANDALISM

Unfortunately, many community gardeners are confronted with vandalism or theft. Where plant theft is a problem gardeners sometimes resort to using locks and chains around the trunks of prized shrubs to make it more difficult for thieves to make off with them. Thorny or prickly shrubs can act as living fences, and a row or border of climate-appropriate raspberry, quince, holly, or firethorn can keep unwanted visitors from more delicate or attractive plants.

With plants such as roses, tomatoes, and herbs it might be best to plant extra to account for some "shrinkage." The week before Mothers Day is high season for thieves who do their "shopping" at the expense of community gardeners. Waiting until after Mothers Day to put in attractive plants may make the difference in whether they remain in the community garden or end up in someone else's garden or vase. Involving neighbors in the garden through events and activities can bolster pride of ownership and deter vandalism, particularly youth. See the chapters on fostering community (page 100) and youth garden programs (page 36) for more ways to engage neighbors.

Making environmentally sound choices in a community garden is not easy, but it is possible. Zero waste, zero nonrenewable energy input, conservative water use, and seed saving are all achievable goals. Healthy leadership, clear rules, and community engagement are just as important. The harvest is great food, a beautiful environment, and close-knit communities.

# Soil Health and Safety

## Ulrich Lorimer

Any successful garden begins with soil, and soils in developed areas with a history of disturbance present a range of challenges for community gardeners. They often have to deal with construction rubble and concrete, soil compaction, nutrient-poor soils, and soil contamination. Besides the obvious challenge of removing garbage and construction debris, excess concrete residue can change a soil's pH over time. (Most concrete is made with limestone, which, as it breaks down, makes the surrounding soil more alkaline, to the detriment of many garden plants that favor neutral to slightly acidic soils.) Heavy vehicle and foot traffic lead to soil compaction, a condition in which the pore spaces in the soil are compressed, restricting water and mineral movement and retention. Frequently, nutrient-poor subsoil is used as fill after construction projects are completed. And, depending on the specific site history, the soil may be contaminated with heavy metals such as lead.

The good news is that there are a number of simple practices that community gardeners can follow to rebuild their soil's structure and health. The key is to know what challenges your garden faces.

## Analyzing Your Soil

The first and most important step to take before anything gets planted is to have your soils analyzed by laboratory professionals. Soil tests can be performed by county cooperative extension offices or private laboratories. The cost for a full analysis generally falls between $15 and $25; some municipalities offer free testing programs. When you order a test, you will usually receive a kit in the mail containing an information sheet and sample bag. (You can also use clean plastic zipper-lock bags for your samples.) Tests are usually completed six to ten working days after receipt of the sample. The results are confidential unless you have otherwise specified. Some labs will archive the data from your soil test for up to five years, allowing you to track changes over time.

### COLLECTING A SOIL SAMPLE

Soil tests should be performed every two to three years and can be taken at any time of the year. Avoid collecting samples when conditions are very wet or when the ground is

**Emeryville Community Organic Gardens in Emeryville, California, uses raised beds filled with healthy soil for plantings.**

**Because many families grow foods in community gardens, it is prudent to know what is in the soil.**

frozen. Use clean, sterilized, and nongalvanized tools to obtain your soil sample (galvanized tools contain zinc and may affect test results). A soil probe or auger is the preferred tool, but a spade or shovel will also work. The sample should be at least half an inch thick and about one inch in diameter, taken from two to ten inches below the soil's surface. If you will be growing deep-rooted crops, you can sample from different depths; be sure to label each depth accordingly and keep samples in separate bags.

It is very important that you get a representative profile of your entire garden. This can be achieved in two ways. The first method is to take several individual samples from various spots in the garden (sunny, shady, wet, dry, etc.) and send them separately. Most soils are not uniform in their characteristics, and this method allows you to collect specific information on various areas. The second method will provide an average reading of your soil. Sample several different areas and combine all the samples in a bucket (avoid metal buckets, which are often galvanized). Thoroughly mix the soil you have collected and then submit a single composite sample to the testing facility.

Never send a wet sample. If your soil is damp, spread it out on a piece of aluminum foil and let it air dry, or set it in an oven at low heat. (If you are testing for soil biology, do not oven dry or you'll kill any organisms living in the soil.) Be sure to include as much information as possible about the site, the types of crops you wish to grow, and any other pertinent details to the testing facility. The information sheet included in the test kit will have extensive questions about your sample site. The more information you provide, the better the testing agency will be able to make recommendations.

## SOIL TEST RESULTS

The laboratory report will include specific results of a number of tests, an interpretation of whether they fall within normal guidelines, and cultural recommendations to address any concerns that have been identified. Many reports provide both "natural and organic" and "synthetic chemical" fertilizer alternatives and cover the following:

• **Soil type and structure.** Soil structure affects the availability of water and oxygen as well as other essential nutrients.

- **Soil fertility.** A number of nutrients are essential for plant vigor and productivity, including macronutrients such as nitrogen, phosphorus, and potassium and micronutrients like copper, iron, and zinc.
- **Soil pH.** Vegetable crops grow best in a slightly acidic soil (pH 6.5 to 6.8).
- **Heavy metals.** Be sure to order a report that will identify levels of heavy metals such as lead, cadmium, and arsenic.

## Heavy Metals and the Urban Garden

In nature, lead occurs at levels between 15 and 40 ppm (parts per million). The World Health Organization has set a permissible lead level in residential and cultivated soils at 100 ppm. The Environmental Protection Agency (EPA) considers levels exceeding 1000 ppm legally hazardous. Since heavy metals are not biodegradable they remain a long-term problem, and lead poisoning in particular is a serious concern for community gardeners.

Heavy metals act as neurotoxins; over time even minute amounts can cause neurological and cognitive problems. Lead blocks calcium absorption and interferes with bone formation. It also decreases muscle strength; large doses lead to wrist and foot droop, among other debilitating conditions. Those most susceptible to lead poisoning are children under the age of six, due to their relatively small body weight and the fact that they are still undergoing bone and neurological development. And because of the

## THE HEALING POWER OF COMPOST

You cannot go wrong by adding organic matter, in the form of good compost, to your soil. Compost is full of beneficial microbes and fungi that condition your soil in a number of ways. Beneficial soil critters will help to mitigate pH problems, vastly improve the water and nutrient retention capability of soil by relieving compaction, add much-needed nutrients and minerals, and most important, begin to break down toxins and contaminants—including heavy metals. Compost is easy to make. A compost bin in your community garden offers a great way to recycle leaves and garden waste into beneficial humus. Add one to two inches of finished compost to your soil in the fall; the organic materials will improve the soil's texture and drainage, and their nutrients will be absorbed into the soil. Over time, regular additions of compost to your garden will greatly improve overall soil health and make your plants happier and more productive. See bbg.org/compost for more about compost.

way children at that age play, they are more likely to ingest contaminated soils. Lead poisoning has been shown to reduce a child's ability to inhibit responses of excitement, causing poor impulse control, distractibility, and impaired reaction time. Exposure to lead by women of childbearing age is also of concern since lead can be directly transferred across the placenta to the unborn child. In short, lead can cause serious and irreversible damage to those exposed to it. Most cities conduct lead-screening programs for young children; check with your local health department or municipality for details.

The primary danger of heavy metal exposure for vegetable gardeners is the deposition of particulates and dust on the outside surface of the plants. This is why washing vegetables before eating is of the utmost importance. However, many vegetables can accumulate heavy metals within the plants themselves. Root crops like carrots, beets, potatoes, rutabaga, and turnips and leaf crops such as cabbage, kale, and broccoli fall into this category. The best way to avoid any accumulation of heavy metals in these crops is to grow them using fresh, clean soil in raised beds or containers, thereby avoiding the original soil all together.

## Safe Gardening Practices

There are a few simple things you can do to help minimize exposure to heavy metals in your community garden.

### PREPARING YOUR SITE

- **Remove and properly dispose of all refuse** and garbage from the site before planting. Look out for old painted wood, tires, galvanized metal, and batteries.

- **Locate food beds** as far away from streets and building foundations as possible.

- **Erect a fence** or plant a hedge to shield vegetables from airborne residues.

- **Keep the soil pH between 6.5 and 6.8.** When soils are slightly acidic, lead becomes less bioavailable to plants. If the soil is too acidic, however, add lime as needed based on soil test recommendations.

- **Condition the soil with organic matter** such as compost and mulch. Not only will this improve the soil in general (see sidebar, page 97), but the organic compounds found in compost will bind with lead and make it less available for uptake by plants.

- **Contain unsafe particles** by covering all bare areas with mulch, straw, or woodchips. This is particularly important on areas of foot traffic such as paths. Stone, gravel, and landscape fabric are also acceptable, but they're less desirable since they do not add any organic matter to the soil.

- **If soil tests show lead levels exceeding 100 ppm,** do not use the soil to grow vegetables. Crops with edible fruits (like tomatoes, peppers, and squash) may be an option—lead does not accumulate in fruit or seeds.

## LIMITING EXPOSURE TO CONTAMINANTS

- **Wear gloves when gardening.** Be sure to wash hands, especially children's.

- **Supervise children** at all times to make sure they don't eat any soil or unwashed vegetables. Your garden may wish to create a safe play area to keep children happily occupied in one place.

- **Keep boots, tools, and contaminated clothing out of the house.** Reducing the amount of soil and dust in the home can reduce the exposure to contaminants by young children. Remember, toddlers like to crawl around and are therefore at greater risk if there is a lot of soil or dust on the floor. Periodically wash outdoor toys as well.

- **Wash all vegetables thoroughly before eating.** Try using a solution of water and vinegar or liquid dish soap (about one teaspoon vinegar or a half teaspoon dish soap to one quart water).

- **Consider growing leaf and root crops in containers** or raised beds with fresh, clean soil in which accumulation of heavy metals is not a concern.

Share this information with other community gardeners as well as with your neighbors and colleagues. Awareness, sound garden design, and long-term planning will keep children and gardeners safe from heavy metal contamination.

**Soil-isolation techniques such as raised beds can be used to grow vegetables in areas where there is inadequate soil. Use natural building materials (treated wood may contain arsenic) and fresh, uncontaminated soil from a known source on top of a barrier such as landscaping fabric. Red Hook Community Farm in Brooklyn (pictured) was constructed over a paved area.**

FOOD BANK GARDEN

THE GIVING GARDEN

GREEN SPOT

Adam Rogers Park Community Garden "Our Serenity under the Sun"

This is a community garden. For information and plot availability call S.L.U.G.

Time began in a Garden

WARREN G. MAGNUSON PARK

CHILDREN'S GARDEN

# Bringing Community Into the Garden

## Robin Simmen

> In order for a garden to be sustainable as a true community resource, it must grow from local conditions and reflect the strengths, needs, and desires of the local community. —*Growing Communities Curriculum*, American Community Gardening Association

A community garden is a place born of collaboration and cared for by its neighbors. Unlike a park built and maintained for the public, a community garden is designed by the public. It succeeds over time only if it reflects local ideas about shared open space. Community gardens depend on people, not institutions, for the energy to continue. They must be inclusive and nurture neighborhood interests and values, or they lose the vital sap that keeps them alive: everyone's deep desire for a village green that gives people a special sense of place.

Community gardeners have to work hard to make sure their gardens don't seem like exclusive clubs. When space is limited, it takes effort for gardeners to find ways to invite everyone who might have daily access to the garden to come and enjoy it. What gardeners need to remember is that reaching out benefits the garden, too. Being inclusive is the only way to ensure a garden's longevity—by making it a resource that the community depends on, supports, and protects.

## Designing Gardens That Include People

**Engage a community when the garden is still just an idea.** This is a great time to take inventory of all the community assets a neighborhood has to offer. Start with the people who live there; they have a wide range of gifts beyond gardening know-how that can be put to great use. Such skills as carpentry, writing, party planning, cooking, child care, herbalism, web design, teaching, performance, driving, and much more can bring people into a community garden project. A good way to tap a neighborhood's resources and find out what kind of garden people would support is to survey their skills and ideas by interviewing them. This process reveals a wealth of information about what people value about their neighborhood, what kind of

**Signage can welcome visitors and confer a sense of place. Clockwise from top left: Magnuson Community Garden at the Warren G. Magnuson Park, Seattle (4); Dowling Community Garden, Minneapolis; Adam Rogers Park Community Garden, San Francisco.**

# PRINCIPLES FOR DOING OUTREACH

The American Community Gardening Association (ACGA) has distilled years of gardeners' experience into a workbook called *Growing Communities Curriculum,* an excellent guide for anyone doing community outreach and development. Workshop outlines and handouts illuminate a list—Growing Communities Principles—for community gardeners, starting with "Engage and empower those affected by the garden at every stage of planning, building, and managing the garden project." Another indispensable outreach resource published by the ACGA is *Cultivating Community: Principles and Practices for Community Gardening as a Community Building Tool.* For these and other resources, visit **communitygarden.org** and **bbg.org/cg.**

garden-based activities would be meaningful in their lives, and what existing community groups could be good partners. Plus, having the opportunity to be heard is empowering and encourages people to get more involved.

**Design a garden that will be of maximum service to the community.** Even though the impetus for starting a community garden might come from a few people wanting to grow vegetables in individual plots, most gardens do well to include a multi-functional area large enough for social gatherings, even at the expense of more beds of plants. Gardens with strong cultural affiliations often construct pavilions or casitas (Spanish for "little houses") in these areas to re-create garden scenes that appeal to the entire neighborhood. If several languages are spoken in a garden, multilingual signs and signs employing universal symbols can help everyone understand important information and also feel more inclusive.

**Accommodate the widest range of potential users.** Many people are physically challenged, and a community garden's design should take this into account. Throughout our lives, we have diverse physical needs. Children need safe areas to play. Older adults appreciate working in raised beds and having easy access to tools and water. Gardeners in wheelchairs require wide, firm paths without barriers. "Universal design" is a broad, comprehensive approach that recognizes a diversity of needs important to all people regardless of their age or ability. Practical universal-design applications in the garden can include raised beds, adequate seating, 36-inch-wide, gently sloped paths, carts for moving plants, and so forth.

**Model sustainability.** Community gardens make great demonstration sites and have been forerunners in educating people about sustainable horticulture techniques, such as composting, no-till planting, solar power, and rainwater harvesting. Gardens advocating these practices do community outreach through workshops, garden tours, signage, and friendly conversation with curious visitors about how to create a greener, healthier planet. By designing efficient three-bin compost systems or installing visible cisterns for storing rainwater for irrigation, these gardens become physical models for sustainable living.

**Offer compost memberships.** Apartment dwellers often have no opportunity to compost their kitchen waste. Compost memberships in community gardens are emerging as a wonderful way to include nongardeners in gardens that have long since filled their individual plots and are looking for ways to expand community involvement. The 6/15 Green Garden in Brooklyn offers a good example of how compost memberships work. Compost members pay a $10 fee (to offset costs of the program, including materials and education) and drop off organic waste and kitchen scraps. They can also work with the garden or the composting program and take compost home throughout the year for their personal use. Composting memberships in community gardens are a real boon for people who want to divert their organic garbage from the world's landfills. By offering their communities places to compost, community gardens perform a service to the environment that adds community value to their garden.

**Display art and showcase the talents of local artists.** Gardens can be designed to feature sculpture as focal points of the landscape and murals as backdrops for the gardens themselves. Painting murals in urban gardens is an especially great way to involve community members who aren't necessarily gardeners. Art installations can also be healing. Witness the transformative power of Lily Yeh's mosaic installations in North Philadelphia, where the Magical Garden sparkles with color and sends peaceful reverberations throughout a neighborhood once wracked with violence.

**Garden tools form a playful trellis at Bradner Gardens Park in Seattle, which also hosts a master gardener program and offers demonstration gardens for Seattle Tilth and Urban Food.**

# ACCESS, FENCES, AND BEYOND

How open is open? Balancing a garden's commitment to being a public resource with its need for being a safe, intact environment is an ongoing challenge for all community gardeners. Most gardens use some kind of fencing to define their boundaries; the height of these fences and the materials used vary widely according to garden needs and resources. Community gardeners agree that there is no perfect, one-size-fits-all solution. Their answers to finding the right fit reflect the different ways communities define themselves and what they opt to tolerate.

## Encouraging Honesty

Community gardens in Seattle are always open. Even though they are fenced and some have gates, they are never locked. "This doesn't mean that we don't have problems, but it goes a long way to show that our gardens are open-space resources," says Sandy Pernitz, community garden coordinator for the city's P-Patch Program. "A certain amount of letting go is necessary since some loss is inevitable," she adds. Sally McCabe from the Pennsylvania Horticultural Society agrees. "Here in Philadelphia we've used every different variation of fencing, and over time one theme has emerged: Fences are smoke and mirrors. Nothing short of landmines will keep out a determined thief who wants your tomatoes."

In New York City, gardens are by and large locked, and gardeners there are mostly astonished by the idea of open gardens. Clinton Community Garden in the Manhattan neighborhood of Hell's Kitchen has come up with a solution that works for its dense urban setting. The garden is designed in two sections: a large parklike area in the front with a locked gate to which 4,000 community members have keys, and a rear allotment garden behind a locked gate to which only gardeners of those plots have access.

Community gardens everywhere benefit from following some simple rules of thumb to discourage theft and vandalism:

- Keep the garden well tended and weed free. A place that looks cared for elicits respect.

- Harvest food as soon as it's ripe. When gardeners go away, make plans to pick each other's produce so that it doesn't tempt thieves.

- Invite people from the neighborhood to come in and harvest when gardeners are there to supervise.

- Plant berry bushes or brambles along the fence with a sign inviting passersby to pick fruit outside the fence.

- Don't plant long-stemmed, commercial-looking flowers; instead grow species with sprays of little flowers. White flowers are stolen less frequently than brightly colored ones.

- Make friends with the people who live nearby and ask them to keep an eye on the garden.

- Report any theft or vandalism to the police, and repair damage right away.

**Family Fun Day at Peralta Hacienda Historical Park in Oakland, California celebrated a community recipe project that brought together Laotian Mien elders and local youth.**

Says Yeh, "Art here is not something to see. Art is the structure of everything I do in transforming the community, in building people, in educating our children. Art is the air that we breathe. Art feeds into our spirit and soul."

**Create viewscapes into gardens to delight passersby.** Well-designed community gardens can provide the whole neighborhood with access to beauty and wonder. Plant flowers or other plants with seasonal interest within view of the public, even if individual plots in the background are screened for privacy. A walk through the Fenway Victory Gardens in Boston epitomizes this experience; visitors wander through a park filled with large allotment plots, each beautifully landscaped. But even a pint-size garden on a busy city corner can offer pedestrians a cooling vision of greenery and a stroll inside during public hours.

## Building Relationships

**Show that community gardeners are invested in the neighborhood.** The garden is living proof that people working together can improve their community, but it is important to take that spirit beyond the garden gate and support the community at large. Community gardeners are rich in the talents, ideas, and relationships needed to build healthy communities, and they are wise to spend time planning how these assets can best be used to make their gardens vibrant resources for community life.

**Develop partnerships with nonprofits.** Before a block association in the Sunset Park neighborhood in Brooklyn created the 64th Street Community Garden, the lot was a garbage-strewn, crime-infested eyesore. Today this garden is thriving, with 50 active members and 9 community groups who use its outdoor classrooms. From the beginning, the garden reached out to local nonprofit partners to get involved and design the space for community purposes. The garden's coordinator Maureen O'Boyle has played a leading role in connecting local schools and agencies—like Brooklyn Youth Court, Caring Hospice (which helped establish a reflection garden), Lutheran Medical Center's diabetic support group, and the New York City Summer Youth Employment Program—to opportunities for learning and healing at the garden. "Getting started with outside groups involves initiating meetings, talking about expectations on both sides, and training volunteers," O'Boyle says. "The benefit is an open green space well used by the community."

## Take Charge of Your Food

Food security and easy access to fresh, nutritious food are of concern to more and more communities across America. Our supply of food is mostly transported from very far away, often from other continents. The lack of grocery stores and greenmarkets in many of our inner cities is partially to blame for chronic malnutrition in underserved neighborhoods. A widespread lack of knowledge about what good food is adds another layer of challenge to addressing these problems.

**Community gardeners are ideally suited to grow food for their communities.** Most community gardens grow food, including fruits, herbs, and vegetables, and some keep small livestock, such as chickens and bees. Many studies have been done on how gardeners significantly improve their diets by consuming garden-raised produce, particularly in low-income neighborhoods. According to GardenWorks, the community garden program of the Green Institute in Minneapolis, urban agriculture in community gardens is three to five times more productive per acre than traditional large-scale farming. Maybe that's one reason why community gardens are able to donate so many tons of fresh produce to soup kitchens and food pantries each year.

**At the Somali Women's Garden at Lawrence Heights Community Centre in Toronto, children learn where food comes from by tending plants.**

**Form farmers' markets to sell organically grown produce at cost to local residents.** Farmers' markets are a huge benefit to communities without adequate grocery stores. Brooklyn has a thriving network of such garden-run farm stands called Brooklyn's Bounty, organized by Just Food, an organization dedicated to developing a sustainable food system in New York City. Gardens are also ideal spots for regional farmers to drop off their food for distribution to local members of community-supported agriculture (CSA) groups.

**Employ the garden as an outdoor classroom for educating children about where food comes from.** (It's not from a box, as so many kids think until they see food being grown.) In response to a powerful wave of consciousness among the young that their food supplies and health are threatened by diminishing green space and that they must learn how to better nourish themselves and their families, youth farms at community gardens are thriving all over the country (see page 36).

## Celebrations and Events for Building Community

What could be more fun than enjoying the breeze with friends at a party on Midsummer's Eve? Or watching outdoor movies, roasting marshmallows, or dancing to live music? The list of excuses to have great garden parties is limited only by the imagination and what is appropriate for the neighborhood. A music festival might not work on a crowded urban block, and a barbecue might be more fun for local residents than a cocktail party. Like everything else about community gardening, these public events often serve many purposes simultaneously: having fun, building something in the garden, membership recruitment, education, and fund-raising.

Community gardens are also wonderful places for private celebrations and rituals such as weddings, christenings, life-partner commitments, birthdays, memorial services, and other life events. Finding a place outdoors for such events is especially difficult in urban areas, and community gardens often function like parks, offering the only green space a neighborhood has. Given the high cost of renting outdoor property for private parties and rituals, a community garden provides a valuable service to the neighborhood when it can accommodate such events, perhaps charging a small fee to cover insurance costs or to raise money for garden activities.

Here is short list of some popular garden events for the whole community:

- **Plant sales and swaps** can provide inexpensive plants for the garden's neighbors as well as the gardeners themselves. Plant sales are great fund-raisers for community gardens as well as good opportunities to recruit new members.

- **Harvest festivals** can celebrate what the gardeners have grown that year and invite the public to learn about heirloom species, related garden crafts such as canning and preserving, and cooking with fresh produce.

- **Post-Halloween pumpkin-smashing parties** for children can be tied to education about composting and recycling.

- **Cooking classes** can be taught by youth as well as seasoned chefs. On a related note, some gardens self-publish cookbooks or market food products prepared from garden produce to raise money.

- **Yoga, tai chi, or meditation classes** can often benefit from a garden setting.

One thing all planners of garden events have in common is the need to get the word out and invite people, whether they are just the gardeners or the whole neighborhood. This is where lots of nongardening skills are useful, such as writing, graphic design, web design, and salesmanship. Putting together a flyer that can be posted at local businesses, libraries, churches, coffee houses, Laundromats, and the like gets the word out to neighbors. Sending a press release to local papers (and following up with photos later!) might be helpful too. E-mail, Listservs, social networking sites, and blogs are used by more and more gardeners to communicate with each other and with others who care about community gardening.

Learning to work cooperatively is the key to staging successful community events. For many people, this means learning new skills and trying out new roles. A big event probably requires the formation of a steering committee at the garden to organize and divide responsibilities for producing it and to oversee any financial

**At Red Hook Community Farm in Brooklyn, a community canning demonstration is offered by Classie Parker (left) and Lorrie Clevenger of the food advocacy group Just Food.**

aspects, especially if recruiting new members or fund-raising is involved. After drawing up a list of tasks to be done, a budget can be agreed upon that describes expenses and any possible revenue. Recruiting volunteers to carry out the workload takes personal follow-up and a very specific description of what is expected of each person who signs up. Preparing a to-do list for the weeks leading up to the event and one for the day of the event with everyone's commitment clearly spelled out is very helpful. This should be distributed to everyone involved to minimize confusion about who's doing what.

A public event at a garden should be seen as a learning process for the whole community, not unlike creating the garden itself. It's important not to expect things to go perfectly but rather to let the event unfold naturally into whatever people make of it, and accept the messy way that our gifts are revealed. Such events help a neighborhood define itself and its values and provide ways for it to express itself. In the end, this is community building at its best, empowering people to discover new relationships as they create healthier, happier neighborhoods.

# Resources

**American Community Gardening Association**

www.communitygarden.org

1777 East Broad Street, Columbus, Ohio 43203

Toll Free: 877-ASK-ACGA

The American Community Gardening Association (ACGA) is a nonprofit membership organization founded in 1979 to help North American gardening programs share their limited resources and thereby benefit from each other's experience and expertise. They offer support, coach fledgling groups, and promote networking and information sharing through an annual conference, local community-building training workshops, teleconferences on topics of interest to community gardeners, and a very active e-mail group. The ACGA also conducts research about and advocacy for community greening. In addition to a quarterly newsletter, the annual *Community Greening Review* handbook, and manuals on community organizing, the ACGA publishes a number of useful articles and tip sheets on their website. The site also hosts a database of community gardens in the U.S. and Canada.

**GreenBridge**

bbg.org/greenbridge

1000 Washington Avenue, Brooklyn, NY 11225

718-623-7250

GreenBridge is the Community Environmental Horticulture Program of Brooklyn Botanic Garden. GreenBridge programs include urban gardener training, a street tree stewardship initiative, the Brooklyn Compost Project, the annual Greenest Block in Brooklyn contest, and the GreenBridge Community Garden Alliance, a network of Brooklyn-based gardens. Resource links and tip sheets on many topics of interest to community gardeners are available online.

**USDA Cooperative Extension System and Master Gardener Programs**

www.csrees.usda.gov/Extension

www.ahs.org/master_gardeners

The USDA Cooperative Extension System is a nationwide educational network that researches and shares information on agriculture, natural resources, and community development. Each U.S. state and territory has a state office at its land-grant university as well as a network of local offices. The Master Gardener program, conducted throughout the United States and Canada, is a leader-training program, in which avid gardeners with an interest in sharing knowledge are provided many hours of intensive horticultural training, after which they contribute at least 40 hours of volunteer service to their community. Master gardeners assist extension offices with garden lectures, exhibits, demonstrations, school and community gardening, phone diagnostic service, research, and many other projects. Together, the programs offer a wealth of practical, regionally specific information and support for gardeners. The links above will help you find your local extension office and master gardener program.

## STARTING AND RUNNING A COMMUNITY GARDEN

**American Community Gardening Association**
www.communitygarden.org/learn
Start-up guide, tip sheets, and many resource links. Be sure to sign up for the ACGA e-mail group and e-newsletter.

**City Farmer**
www.cityfarmer.info/category
  community-gardens
Stories and tips about urban farming from around the world.

**Community Garden Organizer's Handbook**
www.cacscw.org/gardens/handbook
A comprehensive, downloadable manual by the Community Action Coalition for South Central Wisconsin.

**LA County Cooperative Extension Common Ground Garden Program**
celosangeles.ucdavis.edu/garden
A community garden start-up guide, school garden resources and e-mail groups, master gardener training, and more.

## YOUTH PROGRAMS

**Center for Ecoliteracy**
www.ecoliteracy.org

**Center for Food and the Environment LiFE Curriculum**
www.tc.edu/life

**The Food Project**
www.thefoodproject.org

**Garden Mosaics**
www.gardenmosaics.cornell.edu

**National Gardening Association**
www.kidsgardening.com

**School Garden Wizard**
www.schoolgardenwizard.org

## HABITAT GARDENS

**Monarch Watch**
www.monarchwatch.org

**National Wildlife Federation**
www.nwf.org/gardenforwildlife

**North American Butterfly Association**
www.naba.org

## OTHER GARDEN PROGRAMS

**American Horticultural Therapy Association**
www.ahta.org

**Local Harvest**
www.localharvest.org

**National Immigrant Farmer Initiative**
www.immigrantfarming.org

## STRATEGIES

**Composting**
Brooklyn Compost Project
bbg.org/compost

**Natural Gardening**
BBG All-Region Guides
bbg.org/handbooks

**Rain Gardens**
Rain Gardens of West Michigan
www.raingardens.org

**Rainwater Harvesting**
Water Resources Group
www.waterresourcesgroup.org

**Seed Saving**
Seed Savers Exchange
seedsavers.org

**Universal Design**
See the CAC Community Garden handbook.
www.cacscw.org/gardens/handbook

## THERE'S MORE!

For an expanded list of resources for community gardens, visit **bbg.org/cg.**

# Contributors

**Ellen Kirby** is the former director of GreenBridge, the community environmental horticulture program of Brooklyn Botanic Garden. She is a member of the American Horticultural Therapy Association and a member and former president of the American Community Gardening Association. She has a masters degree in theological education and a certificate in horticulture from BBG. For more than 20 years Kirby served as the coordinator of a community garden in Brooklyn; since her retirement from BBG in 2007 she has lived in Brooklyn and Winston-Salem, North Carolina.

**Elizabeth Peters** is the director of Publications at Brooklyn Botanic Garden. She is the former editor of the *Independent Film and Video Monthly* and has written toolkits on grassroots organizing and community building. From 1990 to 1992 Peters coordinated Tuscarora Organic Growers, a collective of small central Pennsylvania family farms that sells fresh, local produce in Washington, D.C.

The **Chicago Botanic Garden** has 30 years' experience working with Chicago-area neighborhoods, schools, churches, and human service organizations to create and maintain gardens. Since 2003, the garden has focused on apprenticeship training and leadership development for high school students through the Green Youth Farm program. **Patsy Benveniste** is vice president of Community Education Programs and oversees the garden's outreach efforts. **Angela Mason**, M.S., is a horticulturist, trained landscape designer, and youth education specialist who manages the Community Gardening and Green Youth Farm programs. **Eliza Fournier**, M.S., is a community garden educator and coordinates the Green Youth Farm program in Chicago's North Lawndale neighborhood. **Lynne Haynor** is a youth development educator who coordinates the Green Youth Farm North Chicago site.

**Susan Fields** is the manager of GreenBridge at Brooklyn Botanic Garden. She formerly served as the deputy director of the GreenThumb program of the New York City Parks Department and worked with community gardens throughout the city. Fields has degrees in social work and psychology, a certificate in gardening from the New York Botanical Garden, and has studied horticultural therapy.

**Garden Cycles** was a three-month documentary project undertaken in 2007 by three young women on bicycles, who toured from Washington, D.C., to Canada to investigate the emergence of the "new American farmer." **Lara Sheets** cofounded the 7th Street Garden education program, which helps address food justice in D.C.'s Shaw neighborhood. **Kat Shiffler** is a freelance journalist whose reporting has been featured in *Z Magazine*, *Clamor*, and *Glimpse* and on public radio. **Liz Tylander** is a community outreach coordinator for D.C.'s Urban Forestry Administration. She has a range of experience in community organizing and natural resource management, and also teaches high school students about their local ecology.

**Lenny Librizzi** is the assistant director of the Open Space Greening Program at the Council on the Environment of New York City. He is one of the founders of the Water Resources Group, which promotes sustainable water practices in community gardens; he is the project developer and leader of NYC's Community Garden Mapping Project; and he teaches the horticulture component of Learn It, Grow It, Eat It, a youth environmental education program. Librizzi is a former board member and publications chair of the American Community Gardening Association and has been actively involved in environmental issues for over 25 years.

**Ulrich Lorimer** is the curator of the Native Flora Garden at Brooklyn Botanic Garden and holds a degree in landscape horticulture from the University of Delaware. He teaches various gardening, native plant, integrated pest management, and botany classes at Brooklyn Botanic Garden and the New York Botanical Garden.

**Aaron Reser** lives in Minneapolis and researches, writes, and illustrates for clients including the Chicago Botanic Garden and Heifer International. She has worked for seven seasons with farmers from around the globe while a grower with Farm in the City in St. Paul, Youth Farm and Market Project in Minneapolis, and the Red Hook Community Farm in Brooklyn.

**Robin Simmen** is director of GreenBridge, the community environmental horticulture program at Brooklyn Botanic Garden; formerly, she was GreenBridge manager. Her work at BBG promotes a greener Brooklyn, community gardens, sustainable horticulture, composting, and soil and water conservation. She previously served as an environmental planner for the Pioneer Valley Planning Commission in Massachusetts, where she focused on land use and water resource issues. Simmen holds degrees in landscape design from Conway School of Landscape Design and Cornell University.

**Marilyn Smith** is director of Children's Education at Brooklyn Botanic Garden. Each year over 150,000 children are reached through the Garden's education programs, and BBG's Children's Garden, established in 1914, gives children ages 3 to 13 direct experience in preparing gardens and tending plants. Smith has worked in the field of environmental education for nearly 20 years. Before coming to BBG, she worked as a naturalist in Ohio and directed a nature center in Connecticut.

**Pat and Clay Sutton** are writers, lecturers, and naturalists who have cowritten several books, including *How to Spot Butterflies, How to Spot an Owl*, and *Birds and Birding at Cape May*. Pat is a founding board member of the North American Butterfly Association and served as program director at the New Jersey Audubon Society's Cape May Bird Observatory for 21 years. Clay is a conservation consultant and longtime instructor for the American Birding Association's Institute for Field Ornithology. They live near Cape May, New Jersey.

**Daniel Winterbottom** holds a BFA from Tufts University and a Master of Landscape Architecture from the Harvard Graduate School of Design. He is an associate professor in the Department of Landscape Architecture and adjunct professor of architecture at the University of Washington, Seattle, where he directs a design/build program through which students work with communities to create design solutions that address social and ecological concerns. Winterbottom's work on casitas, healing gardens, sustainable design, and service-learning teaching has appeared in *Places*, the *New York Times, Seattle Times, Landscape Architecture*, and *Garden Design*; he also wrote *Wood in the Landscape*.

# Photos

# Gardens in This Book

Adam Rogers Park Community Garden, San Francisco

Berkeley Street Community Gardens, Boston

Bethabara, Winston-Salem, North Carolina

Blaine Elementary School, Philadelphia

Bradner Gardens Park, Seattle

Carrie McCracken Garden, Manhattan

City Farmer's Demonstration Garden, Vancouver, Canada

City Slicker Farms, West Oakland, California

Clinton Community Garden, Manhattan

Community CROPS, Lincoln, Nebraska

Community Peace Garden, Minneapolis

Dias y Flores Community Garden, Manhattan

Dowling Community Garden, Minneapolis

East Dallas Community Garden

East New York Farms!, Brooklyn

East York Community Garden, Toronto

Eco-Vida, Chicago

Edible Schoolyard, Berkeley, California

1100 Block Bergen Street Garden, Brooklyn

El Girasol, Bronx, New York

El Sol Brillante, Manhattan

Emeryville Community Organic Gardens, Emeryville, California

Farm in the City, St. Paul

Fenway Victory Gardens (Richard D. Parker Memorial Victory Gardens), Boston

The Food Project, Boston

Food Share, Toronto

Friends of Burlington Gardens (FBG), Burlington, Vermont

Garden of Eatin', Seattle

Gardeners in Community Development, Dallas

GardenWorks, Minneapolis

God's Vineyard Community Garden, New Orleans

GreenBridge Community Environmental Horticulture Program, Brooklyn

GreenThumb Community Gardens, New York City

Green Youth Farm, Chicago

Growing Power, Chicago and Milwaukee

Hattie Carthan Garden, Brooklyn

Heart of Phinney, Seattle

Hope Garden, Dallas

Intervale Center, Burlington, Vermont

Joseph Daniel Wilson Memorial Garden, Manhattan

Karl Linn Garden, San Francisco

Learning Garden, Los Angeles

Lower East Side Ecology Center Garden, Manhattan

Magical Garden, Philadelphia

Magnuson Community Garden, Seattle

Morris Jumel Community Garden, Manhattan

Mr. McGregor's Garden, Dayton, Ohio

Neighborhood Gardens Association, Philadelphia

Nuestras Raíces, Holyoke, Massachusetts

Our Saviour Garden, Dallas

Parkdale Community Beer Garden, Toronto

Pavilion Circle, Cape May, New Jersey

P-Patch Program, Seattle

Phinney Ridge Community Garden, Seattle

Project Grow, Ann Arbor, Michigan

Red Hook Community Farm, Brooklyn

Refugee Community Garden, Boise, Idaho

Riverdale Meadows Community Garden, Toronto

Schwab Rehabilitation Hospital, Chicago

6BC Botanical Garden, Manhattan

6/15 Green Garden, Brooklyn

Sixth Judicial District Community Supervision and Correction Department of Lamar County, Texas

64th Street Community Garden, Brooklyn

Somali Women's Community Garden, Toronto

Soo Line Community Garden, Minneapolis

South End Lower Roxbury Open Space Land Trust, Boston

Southside Community Land Trust, Providence, Rhode Island

Strathcona Community Allotment Garden, Vancouver, Canada

Sunshine Community Gardens, Austin, Texas

Troy Gardens, Madison, Wisconsin

Urban Oasis, Brooklyn

Wasatch Community Gardens, Salt Lake City

Yesler Terrace garden, Seattle

Youth Farm and Market Project, Minneapolis

# Index

# PROVIDING EXPERT GARDENING ADVICE FOR OVER 60 YEARS

Join Brooklyn Botanic Garden as an annual Subscriber Member and receive our next three gardening handbooks delivered directly to you, plus *Plants & Gardens News*, *BBG Members News*, and reciprocal privileges at many botanic gardens across the country. Visit bbg.org/subscribe for details.

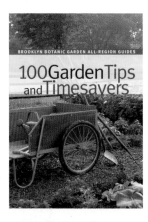

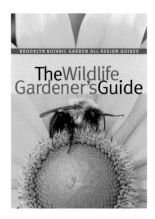

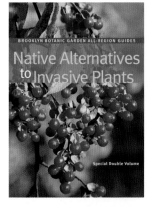

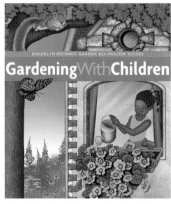

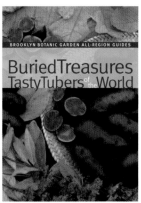

## BROOKLYN BOTANIC GARDEN ALL-REGION GUIDES

World renowned for pioneering gardening information, Brooklyn Botanic Garden's award-winning guides provide practical advice in a compact format for gardeners in every region of North America. To order other fine titles, call 718-623-7286 or shop online at shop.bbg.org. For additional information about Brooklyn Botanic Garden, call 718-623-7200 or visit bbg.org.